MOSBY

GRAY GHOST OF THE CONFEDERACY

MOSBY

Gray Ghost of the Confederacy

BY

JONATHAN DANIELS

ILLUSTRATED BY ALBERT ORBAAN

J. B. Lippincott Company

PHILADELPHIA AND NEW YORK

Contents

MOSBY

GRAY GHOST OF THE CONFEDERACY

Boy with a Pistol

"I'm going to eat him blood raw."

George Turpin, a big tough medical student sent that message to slender, delicate John Singleton Mosby at the University of Virginia in Charlottesville in the spring of 1852.

John Mosby was only nineteen. He looked not at all like a man who would become the most feared and hated of the partisan raiders of the Confederacy. He weighed a little over a hundred pounds; it would have seemed incredible then that he would delay and disrupt great Union armies. His specialties, which sometimes showed up later in his reports of his exploits, were Greek, Latin and literature. He seemed to know much more about poetry than partisan fighting.

Still, when he got the message that Turpin meant to "eat him up," he put in his pocket a pepperbox pistol. That was an early type of automatic gun with a series of revolving barrels fired by one trigger. He did not seem disturbed. He went to a test in mathematics which was his most difficult subject. This day, however, he did his problems easily and well. Then, armed, he went back to his boarding house for dinner. He was ready.

The faculty of the university and the townspeople of little Charlottesville, in 1852, had grown impatient with student violence. Perhaps young men had behaved no worse at the University of Virginia than at other colleges in those lively days. Some felt, however, that the boys had carried too far the notions of the college's founder, Thomas Jefferson. He believed that in their human rights young men should be restricted by few academic or other disciplines. So, along the serpentine walls and under the shaded arcades of the beautiful college in the quiet town among towering hills, misbehavior was common. Flaming firecrackers were flung at the doors of professors' houses. There was much drinking and gambling. The college bell was often rung in the middle of the night. Loud and not always elegant song awakened sleeping citizens. Young men raced teams of blooded horses through the college grounds. Pistol shots were frequently heard.

Some improvements had been made. An honor system was put into effect in 1842. Still the patience of teachers and townspeople was very limited when John Mosby, a sandy-haired boy not quite seventeen, came from his father's farm nearby, on October 3, 1850, to enroll. He seemed mild and frail. Studiously he applied himself to his courses. In the classics he made distinguished marks. He passed his English ahead of schedule. Then in his second year, on March 29, 1852, he shot the big, threatening Turpin and aroused the college and the town.

It was never quite clear what the fight was about. Some said a girl was involved. Another version was that when John invited some boys to a party at his father's house, Turpin had sneered that he invited some of them not as guests but as unpaid fiddlers. Whatever the cause, the tall Turpin was no one to quarrel with carelessly. He had already stabbed one fellow student with a pocket knife and almost murdered another with a rock. Still John, as a slim, stoop-shouldered student, was not angelic. He had a reputation as a fighter, too.

John waited at his boarding house. At dinnertime he went up a narrow staircase from the dining room in the basement and found Turpin there. Then, so one account

of the affair went, young Mosby shouted at the medical
student, "I hear you have been making some assertions—"
and fired before he finished the sentence. John claimed
that Turpin was springing upon him when he shot. Certainly when the witnesses poured up from the dining room,
John, with smoking pistol in hand, was bending above
Turpin. The big medical student lay on the floor with a
bullet through his throat and jaw.

The shooting aroused the authorities. Fortunately for

John, Turpin's wound turned out not to be serious. Still young Mosby spent two months, awaiting trial, in the dark and dirty jail of the little town. Then the prosecutor, William J. Robertson, later famous Virginia judge and attorney, pressed for stern punishment. The jury did not seem so eager. It came back once for instructions. Finally, it found John guilty not of "malicious shooting" as charged, but of "unlawful shooting." It recommended twelve months in jail and a five-hundred-dollar fine.

Suddenly then, sympathy shifted to John. In the jail he made friends even with his prosecutor. Smiling, he jokingly told the lawyer that he was reading *Paradise Lost* and hoped soon to be reading *Paradise Regained*. Also, when he said that he planned to study law, Robertson lent him books from his own library. Nine of the jurors who convicted him joined three hundred other citizens in petitioning the Governor to pardon the young man. Not only did the Governor free John, but the Legislature also rescinded his fine. One thing which influenced everybody was a certificate, signed by several respected doctors, that as a constitutional consumptive, John was so frail that imprisonment for a year would endanger his life.

That delicate constitution was not news to John or his friends. As a child, he wrote later, he "often heard that I would never live to be a grown man." He was raised as a frail little boy. When he was born in Powhatan County, a little west of Richmond, on December 6, 1833, his mother, Virginia McLaurine Mosby, had already lost one child in infancy. As wife of Alfred Daniel Mosby, graduate of Hampden-Sydney College and a slave-owning farmer, Virginia petted and guarded her boy. When he started to school, an older Negro boy always accompanied him. John was not only slight but sensitive. He was deeply distressed one day when older boys pretended to sell his Negro companion at a mock slave sale. He was shocked when on another day he saw his schoolmaster down drunk in the road. Mosby never defended slavery and the only thing he liked about liquor was that sometimes it befuddled those sent out to catch him.

Perhaps the spectacle of the schoolteacher in the road led John's father to secure as teacher for his younger daughters a prim, Yankee schoolmarm from Massachusetts. Her name was Abby Southwick. Friend of such ardent abolitionists as William Lloyd Garrison and Wendell Phillips, she was outspoken in her own strong views about slavery. Yet, the slave-owning Mosbys all loved her and she loved them. Years later, at the end of the Civil War, she sent money and supplies to her old friends in the ruined South. Also she wrote that during the war, while most of her Northern friends were clamoring for John Mosby's blood, she anxiously read the papers fearing to find that he had been killed.

The delicate boy Abby Southwick remembered showed himself able to take care of himself in other schools he attended as a small boy. Those were days when boys were expected to show their mettle by scrapping. John showed an early readiness to fight—and without regard to the size of his opponents. He remembered that at a log schoolhouse near his father's farm in the hills about the University of Virginia, his teacher there—"a most excellent woman"—sternly and equally whipped him and her own son for fighting.

That was, however, Mosby recalled, the only time he was whipped in school. Perhaps, despite his readiness with his fists, he seemed too delicate for the switch. He was not very active in games. Yet he loved to rove the woods as a young hunter. Also, he began to learn early the excitement to be found in books.

The boy was most impressed in his school readers by pictures of General James Wolfe dying heroically at Que-

bec and of the New England ranger and soldier, Israel
Putnam, galloping down stone steps with the British dra-
goons close behind him. The first book he ever read for
pleasure and not merely for school was *The Life of General Francis Marion.* He never forgot the story of General
Marion, the Swamp Fox, who harried the British for
George Washington.

"I remember how I shouted," Mosby said later, "when
I read aloud in the nursery of the way the great partisan
hid in the swamps and outwitted the British. I did not
expect that the time would ever come when I would have
escapes as narrow as that of Putnam and take part in adventures that have been compared with Marion's."

No such adventures at the head of swift-striking little
bands of brave men seemed in prospect then. John began
to ride or walk down the hills into Charlottesville to study
in a school, conducted by two men who afterwards were
professors under General Robert E. Lee at Washington
and Lee University. He learned to recite Tacitus and
Thucydides, but he read with more delight Washington
Irving's romantic stories of the fighting of the Spaniards
and the Moors in Granada. Young Mosby was a serious
student but he was already stirred with ideas of honor,
adventure and valor before he entered the University of
Virginia. Big George Turpin would have been safer there
if he had understood the militant spirit of the slim boy he
taunted and threatened.

Lawyer Robertson understood John better when he discovered the friendly, eager character of the boy he had
prosecuted. He not only lent him law books in jail, but
after John was released took him into his office to study
law. John did so well that three years later, in October
1855, he went to the boom town of Bristol on the Tennessee line. There, with a hot poker, he burnt into a
shingle the sign: "John S. Mosby — Lawyer." Bristol, tem-

porarily called Goodson after its promoter, had high hopes
as a town where railroads East and West were soon to
meet. It attracted thrifty settlers, as well as some tough
characters who gave it a frontier quality.

John was the town's first lawyer. Business came to him
not only because the town needed a lawyer but because
some of his clients were as pleased by his ready quotations
from poetry and the classics as by his knowledge of law.
He prospered to the extent that, on December 30, 1857,
he was able to take as a bride a pretty Kentucky girl, Pauline Clarke. Neither of them knew then that soon she too,
would require a cool head and courage as wife of a man
whom determined and angry Yankee generals would be
seeking.

Both were aware of the increasing tension about slavery
and secession. Though John made a good friend of the
editor of the local paper who thought secession was in-
evitable, he boldly declared himself as a strong Union man.
That was not a popular position. Prominent citizens
around him were talking more and more of war.

"I shall fight for the Union, sir," he told the editor. He
added that they would meet in arms.

Debate moved toward decision. Much against the
South's wishes, Abraham Lincoln became President. At
Charleston, South Carolinians fired on Fort Sumter. Lincoln called for 75,000 troops to invade the South and sup-
press rebellion. Under such circumstances other Virginians,
notably Robert E. Lee who loved the Union and opposed
slavery, were changing their minds. So it was not strange
when John's friend the editor saw the young lawyer in
"the bob-tail coat of a cavalry private" in the Virginia
army.

"That's not a Federal uniform," the editor said smiling.

Mosby grinned, too: "No more of that. When I talked
that way Virginia had not passed the ordinance of seces-

sion. She is out of the Union now. Virginia is my mother, God bless her! I can't fight against my mother, can I?"

Later John, recalling this meeting with his editor friend, remembered that the editor like some others who talked much of war never appeared in the uniform of either side. He explained his own decision simply.

"Virginia went out of the Union by force of arms, and I went with her."

He would be one of the last to come back. In 1861 he was twenty-eight years old. He had two children and a growing law practice. Furthermore, once in the army, he did not find service at first glance as glamorous as the books had led him to expect. Serving as sentinel in a cold wind, his military ardor was temporarily chilled. He was the most frail and delicate man in the company. Still, he recalled with pride that during the whole first year in which he served as private, he only once missed his duty as a sentinel on the alert three times every week. And that was after he was disabled one night when his horse stumbled over a cow lying in the road.

Greater hazards than that awaited the stoop-shouldered young soldier on the main roads and the by-roads, in the dark woods and the enemy-occupied towns of Virginia.

CHAPTER 2

Join the Cavalry!

"If you want to have a good time," ran the rollicking Civil War song, "Jine the cavalry."

And the lively lines went on from there, often to the accompaniment of a mounted banjo player:

> If you want to smell hell—
> If you want to have fun—
> If you want to catch the devil—
> Jine the Cavalry.

It was not all fun or fury at first for John Mosby. In the Washington Mounted Rifles, as his company was called, his captain was a hard-drilling and loud-cursing old army man named William E. Jones. He had graduated from West Point and fought Indians on the plains. Along the way as he swore and fought he had acquired the appropriate nickname of "Grumble" Jones. He had retired from the army before the war. Now, scorning military trappings, he came to the service of Virginia wearing blue jeans and a hickory shirt. The insignia of his rank was carelessly sewn on the shoulders of his old homespun coat. There was nothing slipshod, however, about the way in which he drilled his cavalry recruits.

In the camp in western Virginia, on the march to Richmond, and in the crowded Confederate capital, slim, sandy-haired Mosby won Grumble's regard. John was proud of the cheers the company received. He was prouder still when Captain Jones growled his good opinion of him. In the poorly armed Virginia forces, the Captain managed to get six of the best short cavalry guns called Sharp's carbines. They would "kill at a thousand yards," John wrote his wife, Pauline. Jones picked the men who got the guns. John was one of them.

"I shall always put these men in front," said the gruff officer. "I shall always place them in the post of greatest danger."

That was where John wanted to be. He saw little action, however, in the Shenandoah Valley where the company was sent to serve under a dashing colonel, named James E. B. Stuart, whose initials gave him the nickname "Jeb." Plain Grumble Jones called Stuart a "whippersnapper." But to John who was a little younger than Stuart, the Colonel seemed just the kind of soldier he wanted to be.

There was nothing homespun about Stuart's dress. Big and bearded, Jeb Stuart rode gaily to war with a dark plume waving on his hat. He wore white buckskin gauntlets. Over his trim uniform, his gray cavalry cloak was lined with scarlet. On his polished boots were little spurs of gold. He always rode the best horses—and rode them so hard that even the best did not last long under his saddle.

Even with tough Grumble and dashing Jeb, John saw little action then. As a young soldier and later as a veteran, he was critical of General Joseph E. Johnston who took over the command in the area from General Thomas J. Jackson. John did not like it when Johnston retreated and gave up Harpers Ferry. It was a strategic area in which he was to see more action later. But John cheered with other eager soldiers when the order came to hurry eastward. Beyond rivers and mountains the war's first big battle was shaping up below Washington at Manassas Junction and along a creek called Bull Run.

"On to Richmond," the North was shouting. And it

looked very much as if the Yankees could carry out that threat. From Washington, politicians and ladies and picnickers rode out in carriages to watch the big Union army end the rebellion quickly. But the Rebs had help coming. Stuart left a few cavalrymen to bluff big Union forces in the Shenandoah Valley. The rest of the Confederates under Johnston and Jackson and Stuart hurried east. Grumble Jones put John at the head of his squadron when it marched sixty miles in two days. At Bull Run, Jackson stood like a "Stonewall" and won that great nickname. The confident Yankees were halted, pushed back, driven in headlong retreat to Washington. The South exulted as if it had won the war.

John Mosby played little part in the victory. As one of the six with the carbines, he was sent forward to look for a lurking enemy. The expected force was not there. Then John and the men with him were pulled back into the reserve, where they stayed. Grumble Jones was furious when the general above him did not pursue the retreating Yanks. And John was so disappointed that, when after the battle he wrote his Pauline, he exaggerated his part in a "perfect storm of shot and shell." He had not even been where he could see the front-line fighting.

John's first injury was an accident. One night on sentinel duty he mistook galloping Confederate horsemen for Union cavalry. He fired. The only damage done was that his own horse took fright, whirled out of control and threw John. He was knocked unconscious. Grumble grumbled but John was up and ready for more. Later he was surprised and delighted when Jeb Stuart picked him at random with three other men to go on a scout. This time Stuart cautioned him about quick shooting. He had a better chance with his carbine when he and a friend, Fountain Beattie, who was to become one of his rangers, met and fought two Yankees in a wood. Still, as the months passed, action along the front so quieted that, in January 1862, Grumble Jones gave him a six-day furlough.

When he came back things began to happen. On February 12, while on picket duty, he watched Stuart, now a general, in his plumed hat and red-lined cape ride into the town of Fairfax Court House followed by an empty carriage. Then, to John's surprise, he was detailed to travel in the carriage with ladies who were retiring to safer quarters behind the front. More surprising still, when he returned after dark in a snowfall, Stuart told him to stay at his quarters that night.

The hospitality troubled John more than danger. Dressed as any common soldier, he was acutely embarrassed in the presence of Stuart and his staff while they sat before a blazing fire and talked unguardedly at dinner and at breakfast.

"I do not think I raised my eyes from my plate, although they chatted freely," John said. But he added, "So here began my friendship for Stuart which lasted as long as he lived."

Stuart apparently knew more about John than John thought. The "common soldier" had scarcely reached his camp before Grumble Jones, who had just been made a colonel under Stuart, asked John to be adjutant of the regiment.

"I was as much astonished," the suddenly commissioned adjutant wrote, "as I had been the night before to be asked to sit at the table with the generals."

He did not like the position very much, however. Ceremonials bored him. Military forms and regulations irked him. When he conducted his first dress parade he was more frightened than in any fight in which he was ever engaged. He was eager to find more exciting duty than that of a ceremonial adjutant. He found it.

As spring came on in 1862, the high hopes of a quick

Southern victory which had followed Bull Run were gone. On the day in February that John became adjutant of the First Virginia Cavalry the Confederates took a bad licking at Fort Donelson in Tennessee from a Yankee general named Ulysses S. Grant. In April the Union Navy captured New Orleans. At Shiloh, Southerners learned bloodily that the Yanks could and would fight.

Now in Virginia new, greater Union forces moved under General George B. McClellan, hailed as the "Young Napoleon." General Joseph Eggleston Johnston drew the Confederate forces back toward the Rappahannock River. But McClellan was also moving an army down the Potomac where he could come up the peninsula between the York and James rivers and take Richmond from the east.

It was not clear where the main Federal force was or where McClellan meant to hit his hardest blow. Stuart, in command of Johnston's rear guard, put the First Virginia Cavalry in position to meet a Yankee attack from the north. The handsome Jeb peered through his field glasses at threatening Yankee troops.

"General Johnston," he said to those about him including Grumble Jones and his adjutant, "wants to know if McClellan's army is trailing us or whether this is just a feint."

Slim John Mosby perked up. He had among his comrades an almost comic reputation for wanting to be first with the news. Somehow he got newspapers from the Yankee side of the line before anyone else did. Getting the news first, one officer said, was his "ruling passion." Now he spoke up.

"Give me a guide," he said to Stuart, "and I'll find out for you."

Jeb Stuart looked for a moment at the young, sandy-haired officer. Then promptly he gave the adjutant a guide who knew the roads in the neighborhood. With the guide and two other soldiers, John set out around the flank of the enemy column before them. He reached its rear while the Yanks were advancing in a noisy show of strength toward the Rappahannock. And behind the Yanks, as they began shelling the Confederates, John found out what Generals Stuart and Johnston wanted to know. The Yankees were making a lot of noise but they were only a small force with no line of communication with Washington. They were masking some other Federal movement.

With the news, John rode nearly all night back to Stuart. Then as he approached the Southern forces a Reb picket stopped him. He covered the returning scout with his gun. For a moment it appeared that John would have to go back or get shot by a fellow Confederate. Finally, he persuaded the Reb sentinel to let him pass. He galloped to Stuart who was momentarily expecting an all-out enemy attempt to cross the Rappahannock. Breathlessly John told the plumed Confederate commander that the only force before him was a curtain of Yankee cavalry which had been left to cover the retreat of most Federals from that field. Stuart hesitated no longer. He hurried his men toward the bluffing Yankees. The muddy, weary Mosby galloped beside him.

"You can have any reward you want," the General shouted to John.

No reward came though Stuart did put John's name for the first time into the Confederate records: "Adjutant Mosby . . . of the First Virginia Cavalry volunteered to perform the most hazardous service, and accomplished it in the most satisfactory and creditable manner." He added that John was "worthy of promotion and should be rewarded."

Instead John lost the rank he had. Under a foolish provision of the Conscription Law just passed by the Confederate Congress, soldiers were allowed to elect their own officers. John described it as "an attempt to mix democracy with military discipline." In the First Virginia Cavalry the men rejected their colonel, tough old Grumble Jones, and picked in his place Lieutenant Colonel Fitzhugh Lee, an able soldier but one John Mosby never liked. John thought this Lee arrogant and humorless. Once, jokingly in southwest Virginia dialect, he reported to Lee in Colonel Jones' absence, "Colonel, the horn has blowed for dress parade."

Lee flared, "If I ever hear you call that bugle a horn, I will put you under arrest."

John saluted but was angry inside. So when Fitz Lee became colonel, he did not care to serve under him as adjutant. Also, he thought any colonel should pick his own adjutant. He promptly offered his resignation. Lee accepted it. John lost his post and his commission. Perhaps not all the fault was Fitz Lee's. John then, according to one who knew him well, was "a rather slouchy rider" who "did not seem to take any interest in his military duties."

This was April 1862, exactly a year after John rode off to war after "jining" the cavalry. It was a bad time for the Confederacy as well as for John. General Johnston was steadily falling back, knowing certainly now that McClellan was preparing to strike on the peninsula between the York and James rivers. Finally he reached a point where McClellan's Yanks were about five miles from Richmond along the sluggish, swampy Chickahominy River. There Johnston fought in the Battle of Fair Oaks or Seven Pines. The battle was indecisive but the important result was that Johnston was wounded and Robert E. Lee succeeded to command.

General Lee did not consider retreat. With Richmond close behind him, only attack would serve. He studied where to strike. The new commander had a hunch that McClellan's right flank stretching westward was unguarded. He needed to be sure and turned to Stuart to get the information. Stuart knew the man to seek it.

He invited Mosby, grown less timid about eating with officers, to breakfast. Stuart had given John a place as a scout without commission on his staff after he ceased to be adjutant of his regiment. And John had rejoiced in the change of jobs. It brought him, he thought, "under the orders of a man of genius," and saved him from being an adjutant forever. Stuart showed his faith in John.

"I want you to have a look at McClellan for me," the General said.

John nodded.

"Take a small party, the smaller the better, and see what he's doing along Totopotomoy Creek. General Lee wants to know if he's fortifying his right."

Within the hour, as a man without a post or a commission, John set out toward the creek along McClellan's right flank. He took only four men with him. They made a good start, then ran into trouble. Yankee cavalry discovered them and chased hot on their heels. Still Mosby found out enough to convince him that for miles McClellan's flank was only guarded by cavalry pickets.

Through the woods and swamps, John hurried back to Stuart. The cavalry leader was sitting in the yard before his headquarters. The weary Mosby lay down in the grass beside the General to tell what he had discovered.

"A martinet would have ordered me to stand in his presence," the scout said later, perhaps thinking of Fitzhugh Lee.

Stuart listened to his story. John had not been able to get through the Union outposts but he was sure a larger force could. He traced with his finger the route which he believed could be followed to cut through the screen of Yankee forces.

"There's nothing to stop you," he said.

Jeb Stuart was excited. He told John to go to the adjutant's office and put down the route and plan on paper.

John brought his report back but Stuart noticed that it was unsigned. He ordered Mosby to sign it. Then thrusting the paper into his pocket, he set off at a gallop for General Lee's headquarters.

Stuart came back with orders from Lee to go the way John had shown was open. Stuart was in high spirits. John was beside the lively, elegant General when he set out with 1,200 picked officers and men from the First, Fourth and Ninth Virginia cavalries and the Jeff Davis Legion. They had two light guns of the Stuart Horse Artillery. Off in the bright dawn, on June 12, they trotted toward Ashland. An officer at the camp asked Stuart when he would be back.

"It may be for years," the General said merrily, "it may be forever."

John rode ahead. He had not had so much fun since he joined the cavalry.

CHAPTER 3

Scout in Prison

Away they went up the road to Ashland, sixteen miles north of Richmond. With John riding ahead, the column moved as if it were on the way to reinforce Stonewall Jackson in the Shenandoah Valley. Then at the little village of Old Church, they came on Union cavalry pickets and then on two squadrons of Yankee cavalry behind them. The gray cavalry charged and routed the men in blue. The only Confederate to die on the raid fell there.

"We could not stay even to give him a hasty burial," John said. But the burial of that man, Captain William Latane, by Southern women in the neighborhood became a well-loved subject of painting and poetry in the Confederacy. He symbolized the young who died. John was the perfect figure of the young who galloped and lived.

Beyond the Yanks' abandoned cavalry camp General Stuart reined his horse. His force was on the flank of the enemy only nine miles from the York Railroad which was McClellan's line of communications. Aroused by the warning of the fight more Yanks would soon be rushing to the road behind the raiders. The Rebs must turn back quickly or ride all the way around McClellan's army. John wanted to go on. He waited anxiously for Stuart's decision. He was relieved when Stuart turned to him.

"I want you to go on some distance ahead," the General told John.

"Very well, but give me a guide."

Proud to be selected for such duty, John dashed off with

two men who knew the roads. Still, Stuart sent him word to go faster and farther ahead. The scout and his guides captured a sutler's wagon filled with the luxuries for sale to Yankee soldiers. And ahead of them on the Pamunkey River they saw a whole forest of the masts of schooners unloading vast quantities of supplies for McClellan.

John put one man on guard at the sutler's wagon. He sent the other back for a squadron to come burn the schooners and their supplies. He galloped on ahead. Alone he captured another sutler and a sentinel. Then suddenly a bugle blared and straight ahead of him he saw a body of Yankee cavalry. It was too late to turn back. So he charged alone shouting commands as if he were leading a large Rebel force. The Yanks broke and ran. And fortunately for John, gray cavalrymen did quickly ride up behind him.

Three days later, having circled the whole bewildered Union army and built a bridge across the Chickahominy before McClellan could send any large force after them, the triumphant Rebs rode into Richmond. The big Union army was made to look silly. Northern confidence was shaken. Stuart was acclaimed in the South. And there was enough glory to bring Mosby's name into the newspapers for the first time.

This was "the grandest scout of the war," John wrote Pauline. "I never enjoyed myself so much in my life."

He brought back horses and equipment, two fine army pistols and a few presents for Pauline. He was hailed as a hero, second only to General Stuart. In his reports General Lee mentioned John with praise. Also Stuart himself gave John a letter to Secretary of War George W. Randolph. The General spoke of John's bravery and service "time and again."

"I am anxious that he should get the Captaincy of a Company of Sharpshooters in my brigade," Jeb wrote.

John presented the letter. Nothing came of it. Perhaps the reason was that in the pressure of events little attention could be paid to such a matter. These were the days just before General Lee launched his first attack as Commander of the Army of Northern Virginia. Using the information Mosby and Stuart had secured for him, Lee brought Jackson down secretly from the Valley. Stonewall was to hit the Union army on its exposed flank while other Rebel forces attacked McClellan's front. John rode with Stuart when the General moved to give cavalry support to Jackson's men.

The sandy-haired Mosby rode and scouted as the fighting moved through the battles at Mechanicsville, Beaver Dam Creek, Gaines's Mill, Savage Station, Frayser's Farm, on to the escape of McClellan's army beyond bloody Malvern Hill.

"McClellan is badly whipped," John wrote Pauline. He himself, however, was still a man without a commission or a regular post. He considered a chance to move to the command of General John B. Floyd whom he had known in western Virginia before the war. Stuart did not want him to go. Still the cavalry leader's efforts to get John a commission failed. So the young scout went to Stuart with another plan.

A few months before, the Confederate Congress had passed a Partisan Ranger Law. It authorized the formation of bands of rangers as either cavalry or infantry. Recruits were to be received into the service on the same basis as other soldiers, with one significant exception. The rangers were permitted to keep property they captured. Such bands presented problems. The South was not countenancing guerrillas. Also, some feared that recruitment of rangers might upset the regular conscription laws.

The fierce, informal, free fighting of such detached

light troops engaged in harassing the enemy appealed to
John. He had read about such fighters in all parts of the
world. Also, he thought that the need for such raiders on
the Union's rear and communications lines had been greatly
increased by the attitude of a new general President Lincoln had brought from the West. That officer, General
John Pope, had come full of bluster to take command of
the forces in the Valley and around Washington. His own
soldiers resented his declaration that where he came from
the Federals had been used to seeing the backs of their
enemies. And he went on to say: "I hear constantly . . . of
lines of retreat and bases of supply . . . Let us discard such
ideas. Let us study the probable lines of retreat of our
opponents, and leave our own to take care of themselves
. . . Let us look before us and not behind."

John Mosby figured that he could work on those lines
of supply which Pope scorned. Also, no general seemed
so to invite such attentions as Pope. Before he came from
the West, while no punches had been pulled in the fighting, on both sides in Virginia there had been a generous,
almost chivalrous, attitude toward civilians. Now Pope
told his army to live off the country. He seized civilians
and issued harsh orders as to their treatment. General Lee
wanted Pope "suppressed." John Mosby believed he could
help in that operation. So he went to Stuart.

"Give me a dozen men," he asked. He smiled satirically.
With them, he told his friend the dashing General, he could
"do for Pope what he would not do for himself, take care
of his rear and communications for him."

Stuart listened to the scout he had praised and who had
won the praise of General Lee.

"I can make Pope pay as much attention to his rear as
his front," John believed. "I can compel him to detail
most of his cavalry to guard his long line of communi-

cations, or turn his commissary department and rear over to me."

Such a proposal for bold dashes appealed to Stuart. But he declined to give John any men. He told him that he was getting his cavalry ready for the active campaign soon to begin. He could not spare any men. However, Stonewall Jackson might be able to give him a few men for such service. So the General gave John a letter to the Valley leader.

With the letter, less than three weeks after the end of the famous Seven Days battles, John set out accompanied only by a clubfooted man who was exempt from military service. Then at Beaver Dam Station on the Virginia Central Railroad, he decided to hurry on by rail and let the man with the twisted foot follow with his horse. On the morning of July 20, while waiting for a train he took off his haversack and lay down to rest in the depot. Perhaps he nodded. Suddenly he was aroused by clattering hooves of approaching cavalry. Before he could run or hide they pounced upon him. At that time Northern troopers could regard John more with amusement than with the anger and fear which he inspired in them later.

"We captured a young Confederate," wrote one of the Yankee officers, "who gave his name as John S. Mosby. He is slight but well-formed; has a keen blue eye and a blond complexion, and displays no small amount of southern bravado in his dress and manners. His gray plush hat is surmounted by a waving plume, which he tosses, as he speaks, in real Prussian style."

John did not mind the description. He preserved it in his memoirs. Still at the moment neither he nor the Yanks who caught him had any notion that his capture at the little depot was to make possible one of the most useful scouts of his career. Though he was briefly locked up in the dirty Old Capitol Prison in Washington, he was soon sent down the river for exchange. He kept his eyes open as a prisoner as he did as a raider. At Fortress Monroe while he waited, he noticed a large number of transports lying in Hampton Roads.

Keeping up his habits as a scout, he soon learned that these were troops of General Ambrose E. Burnside. They had been brought from North Carolina. John realized that if the troops were reinforcements for McClellan, that would mean that that General was preparing to strike at Richmond again from his base on the James River. If they sailed up the Chesapeake, they would be going to General Pope. Then the next Federal blow would come from the north. John knew that General Lee at Richmond needed to learn the Union plan. The young prisoner watched and listened. He discovered that the ship captain who had brought him and other prisoners down from Washington was secretly a Southern sympathizer. The thin prisoner asked the captain to find out where the troops were going. That evening just before John was to be taken up the river for exchange, the captain whispered to him.

"Aquia Creek, on the Potomac," he said. The Federals were concentrating below Washington.

John passed a restless and excited night. Next morning he was the first man off the boat. Then on the hot August day he set out to walk twelve miles to General Lee's headquarters. Almost exhausted, he lay down beside the road. A sympathetic Reb horseman stopped. John told him how anxious he was to get to General Lee. A horse was provided for him. But when he finally reached the office of the Commander-in-Chief, a staff officer looked him up and down. John was roughly dressed, unwashed and unshaven. Despite his statement that he had important information for the General, he was told "in the imperious tone customary with staff officers" that he could not see him.

Baffled and disappointed, John turned to leave. But another of Lee's aides had listened to the conversation. The tired, dirty young scout was told to wait. Then quickly he found himself in the presence of the great Confederate leader. John was awed by the immaculate, bearded General. But there was nothing imperious in the attitude of Lee. Instead, kindly and gently he put the dirty young soldier at ease. John poured out his information. On a map he showed the movement of Burnside's forces to Pope. Then suddenly, with his information given, he feared that the General might not believe him. He was, he told Lee, the John Mosby whose name the General had put in his report of Stuart's ride around McClellan.

"Oh," Lee said, "I remember."

Then the Confederate chieftain asked John on what line he thought the next movement against Richmond would be made. John was flattered by being asked such a question by Lee. He was happy when the General called an officer (perhaps the one who first refused to let in the roughly dressed young man), and told him to have a courier ready to go to General Jackson.

"As soon as Jackson got the news about Burnside," Mosby said later, "he hastened to strike Pope at Cedar Mountain before reinforcements could reach him."

But before the courier was dispatched, John rose to leave. He realized how tired he was. Also he felt a strange sense of gratitude to Lee. He opened his battered haversack and took from it a dozen lemons. Lemons were kept out of Virginia by the blockade, but John had secured these as a prisoner with money a kind Yankee had given him. Lee smiled at the gift but suggested that it would be better to give the lemons to some of the sick and wounded in the hospitals. John shook his head, weary but insistent.

He said good-by and left the lemons on General Lee's table.

Less than two weeks later, never having reached Stonewall Jackson with Stuart's letter or having become the ranger he wanted to be, John was back galloping beside laughing, elegant, hard-fighting Jeb Stuart.

CHAPTER 4

Mosby Gets His Band

With Jeb Stuart, John rode in the race to defeat General Pope before his reinforcements could come up the river. With a young lieutenant named Samuel B. Gibson, who had been with him in the Yankee prison, he had reached the army just in time to meet Stuart headed for the front. The General had come by rail from Richmond, leaving Colonel Fitzhugh Lee, whom John did not like, to bring up the cavalry. Then Stuart's men were to help hit Pope, who seemed to have bottled himself up between the Rapidan and Rappahannock rivers.

John galloped off with Stuart to meet Fitz Lee and the cavalry at the little village of Verdiersville, a few miles from Orange Court House. Besides John and Gibson, only Stuart's adjutant, Major Norman Fitzhugh, and his big Prussian aide, Major Heros von Borcke, and Lieutenant Chiswell Dabney rode with the General that afternoon. As they approached the little town after dark, there were no signs of the expected cavalry. Stuart sent off his adjutant to look for Colonel Fitz Lee and hurry him along.

The others tied their horses to the porch of a house beside the road. The August night was warm and clear. Civilians told them that no Yankees had been seen in the neighborhood for a month. So the little group rolled themselves up in their cloaks and went to sleep. Before sunrise John was awakened by Gibson. That young lieutenant had heard the tramp of cavalry down the road. John thought it was probably Fitz Lee's men. Still, as a man who had been caught napping once, he woke Stuart.

"Gibson and I will ride down the road and see what's there," John said.

They did not go far. In the morning mist it was hard to tell whether the riders they met were friends or foes. But when the riders opened on them with pistol fire all doubts were ended. Unarmed, as John said later, "there was nothing for us to do but wheel and run—which we did—and used our spurs freely." He and Gibson came back shouting, "Yankee cavalry." As they galloped toward the house, they saw Stuart's huge Major Heros von Borcke dash through the front gate and down the road ahead of them as fast as his horse could run.

John did not care for the big German. After the war von Borcke published, Mosby said, a book full of fables in which he described his encounter with the Yankee cavalry that morning "as more wonderful than the feat of St. George and the dragon." At the time, as Mosby put it, "Our ambition was to escape. We ran as fast as we could, but the Prussian ran faster. That was all the distinction he won." C542471 CO. SCHOOLS

Fortunately the firing and the shouts warned Jeb Stuart. He jumped from the porch bareheaded and mounted his horse. It was too late for him to make the gate. He leaped over a fence in the back yard and escaped into the woods.

"But," said John with his twisted grin, "he left his hat!"

Yanks and Rebs both knew that plumed headgear and the General who customarily rode beneath it. It was a trophy worth seizing. More important, the Yankees also captured Major Norman Fitzhugh who had been sent out to look for the missing Confederate cavalry. On him they found a letter from General Lee to Stuart outlining his plan to attack Pope the next day.

With that warning Pope retreated quickly and the first chance to attack him before the reinforcements arrived was lost. The result did not improve John's poor opinion of Fitzhugh Lee. Perhaps unjustly he blamed that officer for his delay in bringing up his cavalry. General Robert E. Lee, Mosby said, "never again had such an opportunity to destroy an army."

John was not at hand when Stuart got his revenge. He did not accompany the General a few days later when Jeb set out on a raid around Pope. But as the General galloped off he passed John.

"I am going after my hat," he told Mosby gaily.

Jeb Stuart got more than that. In a swift attack on Pope's headquarters, he brought off that boastful General's best full-dress uniform coat. More important, he found Pope's dispatch books giving the details of the arrival of McClellan's men to join the growing Federal army. Lee moved quickly to strike again. John rode with Stuart to the great Confederate victory at Second Manassas. A bullet pierced his hat and slightly grazed his head.

On the way to Manassas, at Bristoe Station, John saw the huge supply depot which Pope had told his army should be disregarded. To the ragged, poorly fed Confederates the vast accumulation of Union supplies was a treasure store almost past belief. The streets were lined with warehouses packed with food and clothing. Stonewall Jackson ordered the heads knocked out of the barrels of whisky and then turned his ragged men loose to feast and pillage. They stuffed themselves with rare foods and washed them down with Rhine wine. They grabbed blankets and shoes. When individual soldiers were glutted, wagons were loaded and started back toward the Confederate lines. Then the great depot was put to the torch. Fires rose above it like a volcano.

No little band of rangers, John knew, could take such a prize. Still the massed supplies emphasized the importance of the lines which a few hard-fighting men might harass and interrupt. There was no time for fulfillment of his hopes then. John crossed the Potomac with Stuart in Lee's first invasion of the North. The Confederates crossed expecting to find many friends in Maryland. They sang the new song about "The despot's heel is on thy shore, Maryland, my Maryland." Later ragged Rebs were to revise that song. Then it was to go:

-Oh, Bob Lee's heel is on thy shore,
Maryland, my Maryland—
You won't see your old horse no more—
We'll ride him till his back is sore—
And then come back and get some more—
Maryland, my Maryland.

John Mosby was to help give reality to that version. Now he fought beside Stuart when a great Federal army, under McClellan, came up from Washington to push Lee back toward the Potomac along a little creek called Antietam at Sharpsburg, in September 1862. With Jeb he rode by the batteries on the bloody field where Stonewall Jackson was directing the fire. The slim scout had to be careful as he rode on that field to keep his horse from treading on the bodies of the many dead. Once John dismounted to arrange a blanket under the head of a dying officer. He took a canteen from a dead man to quench the thirst of a desperately wounded young soldier. To the end of his days Mosby remembered as a "model of chivalry" the fevered boy's refusal of the water on that terrible field.

"No," he said, "take it to my Colonel, he is the best man in the world."

The Union claimed a great victory at Sharpsburg. When Lee recrossed the river 10,000 Confederates lay dead and wounded on the field. But the Confederate General had left many dead Federals behind him, too. He still had his army, and his cavalry was ready for a quick return into the North. Indeed, it was a gay time for the cavalry. There was dancing. Regimental bands played. Often the horsemen sang to the music of Stuart's banjo player. Then on October 9, John rode with a column of 1,800 selected men on a raid which carried them all the way to Chambersburg, Pennsylvania. They blew up a supply depot, brought back 1,200 horses and returned through furious Yankees with the loss of only one man wounded and two missing.

In November Mosby rode around the army of McClellan, which had moved back into Virginia. He stood in the bushes near Catlett's Station and watched McClellan give up the command of the Union army to General Ambrose Burnside. Early in December, on a scout near Manassas, John put up such a bold show with only nine men that, as he wrote, he "stampeded two or three thousand Yankees." He served Stuart well on December 13, 1862, when Lee hurled Burnside's great army back across the Rappahannock at Fredericksburg in bloody defeat.

Then early on Christmas morning, Mosby galloped with Stuart in a raid on the defeated Burnside's communication lines around Dumfries, just below Alexandria. They captured many wagons of supplies. They chased a Yankee cavalry regiment from its camp and feasted on its commissary, including its Christmas turkeys. Jeb Stuart, to John's delight, put his own operator on a Union telegraph line and sent a message to the Federal Quartermaster General complaining of the quality of the mules he provided for Stuart to capture.

The cavalry was having its good time. John Mosby was happy as a part of it. The country through which they rode was the area in which John had spent the first year of the war. The raid carried them through Fairfax and Loudoun counties, along the Potomac opposite Washington from Alexandria up toward the meeting of the

Potomac and the Shenandoah at Harpers Ferry. This area was to be the region later unofficially called Mosby's Confederacy. When he rode through it on that Christmas raid with Stuart, John spoke of it eagerly as "a land flowing with plenty."

A good part of the plenty in the country of rolling hills flowed down Yankee supply lines. And the raid on Dumfries made John more than ever sure that a swift-striking and, when necessary, swift-scattering little band could do great and continual damage at the Yankee rear. Its activities would pin down Yankee troops, which might otherwise be used at the front, to guard the lines behind it. Leading in such fighting had become an obsession with John. He had spoken to Stuart about it twice. Now he went to him a third time.

Resting in the midst of the raid, the gay General made his headquarters for the night at the house of a Colonel Rogers in the village of Dover in Loudoun County. Early in the morning John went up to Stuart's room. He made his request again.

"I asked him to let me stay behind for a few days with a squad of men. I thought I could do something with them."

The gallant Stuart must have realized then that he could deny John no longer. Also Burnside had been defeated. Winter and mud would delay any reorganized and reinforced return of the Yanks to battle. The General regarded John, who had served him so well on so many occasions. Mosby had just passed his twenty-ninth birthday; Stuart himself was not quite thirty then. Jeb listened to the thin, wiry scout. He studied him, too. The slight stoop in Mosby's back was not ungraceful. He carried his chin well forward. His lips were thin. His smile was habitual but a little ironical. His eyes flashed as he talked to Stuart. Yet he looked like no thundering warrior. He seemed shorter than his height of five feet nine or ten. Unbearded, he was youthful and pleasant-looking. But nobody knew better than Stuart how boldly he could fight.

This time Stuart agreed. John got nine men including his old friend and messmate, Fountain Beattie, who had entered the war with him in the Washington Mounted Rifles under old Grumble Jones. The little band stayed behind as Stuart's column turned back toward its head-

quarters at Culpeper Court House. The cavalry rode off with a jangle of sabers on stirrup-irons. Perhaps Stuart looked back at the men remaining in the enemy's country.

Standing beside the road John wore his gray uniform and a brown hat with a dark plume and a golden cord. He carried no saber. Already it seemed a useless, obsolete weapon to him. At his belt he wore two Colt revolvers. He smiled after the cavalry. He was ready to make enemy country his own, his native land. It would not be long before its roads and its towns would resound with the clatter of the hooves of his horses and, among the Yankees, the terror of his name.

CHAPTER 5

Mosby's Men

John did quickly what he told Stuart he could do. Riding with his big guns at his sides, he struck swiftly at Union picket posts in the Virginia counties opposite Washington. Yankees there had not heard a gun shot in months. The area had been in easy Union possession since General Joe Johnston had retreated in the first year of the war, except briefly when Lee passed on his way to Maryland. Union soldiers there had had an easy, lazy life. The situation was summed up in a regular nightly report to the Northern press: "All quiet along the Potomac."

"I saw that here was a bountiful harvest to be gathered," John said, "and that the reapers were few."

He did not think many were required. With his little band of men he roared down on seven New York cavalrymen playing cards by their campfire near Herndon Station. They surrendered. Then a couple of miles away the partisans surprised and captured five Vermont men. Two nights later John and his band took more men and horses at Frying Pan Church.

On January 15, 1863, Mosby and his tired, muddy men rode into the Confederate cavalry camp near Fredericksburg. In two weeks they had captured twenty-two Yanks and their horses and equipment. They had also put an end to the quiet along the Potomac. Jeb Stuart was delighted.

John smiled. "I could do more with more men and more time," he said.

"You shall have them," the General promised.

From the ranks of his old First Virginia Cavalry John was given fifteen men. Some of them had entered the army with him in the old Washington Mounted Rifles under Grumble Jones. Now again Colonel Fitzhugh Lee irritated John. He did not want to let the men go. The Colonel was not alone in his doubts about John's chances. Indeed, Mosby knew that in the whole Army of Northern Virginia, except for two or three of the men who rode with him and knew him well, General Stuart was the only man who believed he could accomplish anything.

In the country crowded with Federal troops the odds seemed certainly against him. The Yanks knew the lay of the land almost as well as he did. He had never been in that area before the beginning of the war. Still, he knew that the region between the Rappahannock and the Potomac rivers was a rich, green land from which his horses and men could secure their forage and food. Many friendly Southerners lived there. In it were great houses and plantations of friends and relatives of Robert E. Lee, and other aristocratic Virginians. As a young man George Washington had tramped and fought in this country. Yet it was also a country in which some Southerners sided with the enemies of the South out of conviction or for a chance to profit from their perfidy.

The Blue Ridge on its western border provided safe places in which Mosby's men could retreat if superior forces were brought against them. The land possessed such forests as covered Robin Hood's merry men. And yet John said there was no such shelter as his Revolutionary hero, General Francis Marion, had found in the swamps of the Pee Dee River in South Carolina.

Still John believed that he could hide and hunt and make the Yanks guard a hundred points while he selected any one of them for attack.

As soon as Stuart gave him his men, he crossed the Rappahannock at Fox's Mill, and headed northward. At the Norris Tavern in Warrenton he stopped for a few hours, but friendly Southerners there only shook their heads at his folly. He led his men on in the night as a cold rain fell. Then in enemy territory he halted close to the Bull Run Mountains.

There he gave the order which was to be basic to his whole plan. He wanted no camp which the enemy could attack. Singly or at most in pairs, the men were to find friendly homes in the neighborhood, stay out of trouble and keep out of sight. They would meet ten days later at Mount Zion Church, on the Little River turnpike a mile and a half east of the village of Aldie in Loudoun County.

"Scatter for safety," he said, "and gather at my call like the Children of the Mist."

At the church on the turnpike on January 28, the men assembled before sunrise. Mosby had spent the time since he dispersed them studying the lay of the land. He had found a man who knew the country better than almost anyone else in it. As one of Mosby's first recruits, John Underwood was certainly among his best. A forester with a thick shock of white hair, Underwood seemed to know every rabbit path in the area. By day or night he could lead the way across open fields, through forests, by the most secret routes to appointed places. John described the quiet forester as a man "equally at home threading a labyrinth of pines in Fairfax or leading a charge."

Now in daylight by sheltered ways, the white-haired forester led Mosby and his men toward Frying Pan Church where John and his first little band had captured Yanks earlier. This time they found only two pickets. Without firing a shot, Mosby took them and rode on to Old Chantilly Church. Following Underwood they crept through the woods toward the church where he said there was a picket post of nine Federal cavalrymen. Nearby they halted.

Mosby crawled forward through the wet woods, then came back with his orders. He and Fount Beattie were to rush two sentinels. As they grabbed them, the others were to charge in, making all the noise they could. The surprise was complete. Only one Yank was shot in the fight. The others surrendered quickly. All their horses and equipment were taken. John divided the spoils as he always did, this time giving Underwood the best horse. That was in accordance with his rule that the men who fought best got most. He himself never asked for or took anything.

Now quickly, however, he won the galloping fury of the Federals. His raids, under the nose of the Union capital and the troops guarding it, seemed not only bold but impertinent. Panic spread in the outposts. At Fairfax Court House, Sir Percy Wyndham was outraged. That Britisher, now a Union colonel, was in command of the Yankee cavalry defending Washington. A proud officer, he had won fame in the Crimean War and later as a soldier of fortune fighting with Garibaldi in Italy. In this country he had been much praised for his exploits in the Union army. And now a little upstart with a ragged band was picking off his men and taking his horses. Wyndham thought he knew more about cavalry than Mosby would ever learn. He set out to show it.

High and proud at the head of two hundred of his horsemen, Sir Percy galloped into Middleburg the next afternoon. Wyndham's information about Mosby's whereabouts was not far wrong. As the Britisher camped for the night on the outskirts of Middleburg, Mosby and Fount Beattie were having a quiet supper with a friendly gentleman, Lorman Chancellor, at his house between Middleburg and Dover. Warned by the clatter of Wyndham's cavalry, the two partisans grabbed their cloaks and galloped off to find others of their band. As the Yanks marched out of Middleburg in the morning, they were watching from hilltops. Then boldly with only seven of his men Mosby attacked the rear of the Englishman's column. They captured a Union rider and three horses.

Perhaps Mosby had been too rash. Enraged, Wyndham wheeled and ordered a pursuit. Three of Mosby's men were captured when their horses fell, among them Fount Beattie. John himself escaped to stand silhouetted on a hilltop, a mocking plumed figure as the furious Wyndham marched away.

The British knight determined to come back. He was outraged by the attack on his rear, which seemed to him improper cavalry tactics. John grinned at what he regarded as Wyndham's knowledge of the "old rules of the schools." He himself, he said, fought "for success and not for display." He laughed at the romantic saber as a cavalry weapon, preferring big pistols. Still he was angered when the spluttering Englishman declared that Mosby was not a partisan but a "horse thief."

Smiling slow and hard John sent him word: "All the horses I had stolen had riders and all the riders had sabers, carbines and pistols."

Since he left Stuart, Mosby had captured nearly twice as many men as were in his band and more than twice as many horses. That could not go on, Wyndham announced. In Middleburg he seized citizens as hostages and threatened to burn the town. Some frightened people asked Mosby to stop his raids. The slender partisan declined to "make any such degrading compromise with the Yankees." He was sorry some of his men had marched captured Yankees through Middleburg. But he added:

"My attacks on scouts, patrols and pickets, which have provoked this threat, are sanctioned both by the customs of war and the practice of the enemy; and you are at liberty to inform them that no such clamor shall deter me from employing whatever legitimate weapon I can most efficiently use for their annoyance."

No such protest ever came from loyal Southerners again. Despite Yankee threats, men and women housed and hid his partisans. They brought him information. They laughed at the jolts he gave and the jokes he played on the Yankees and their few Southern collaborators. Now, however, he had more troubles from another source. Fitzhugh Lee, who grumbled more about Mosby than Grumble Jones ever had, demanded the return of his soldiers.

"So I had to send them back to him," John said.

That did not mean an end to his raids: far otherwise. Soon afterward he reported to Stuart that he had twenty-seven men with him when he hit the Yanks again. His company was growing. Reports of his raids not only angered the Yankees but also elated the Rebs. The hope of spoils attracted some. Men came to get horses so they could go back mounted to their cavalry regiments. But the real appeal of service with him, Mosby believed, was a fascinating life. Its attractions far more than counter-balanced its hardships and dangers. His men had no camp duty which, he said, expressing his own feeling about such routine chores, "is disgusting to soldiers of high spirit." To put them to such work, he added, was "pretty much like hitching a race horse to the plow."

"Old men and boys had joined my band," he reported. "Some had run the gauntlet of Yankee pickets, and others swam the Potomac to get to me. I mounted, armed and equipped my command at the expense of the United States Government."

When he could not pick the men he wanted, he took those he could get. A good many wounded Rebs had been left behind in a Confederate hospital in Middleburg after the fighting in Maryland. Mosby used them. And when the Yanks came searching for his men they never suspected that the hobbling cripples they saw in the daylight were riding and fighting with Mosby at night.

"At last," John said, "I got one of the cripples killed and that somewhat abated their ardor."

As time went on, however, he attracted notable fighters. Mosby himself liked the diverse quality of his band. It was, he said, using one of his frequent literary allusions, "almost as motley a crowd as Falstaff's regiment." Certainly there were characters in his band as varied as some of those who gathered around Robin Hood. Beattie was his faithful companion. Underwood, the forester, was always quietly dependable. There was the brave Dick Moran with a voice which sounded like a foghorn above all fighting. Then came William Hibbs, a huge, brawny, gray-haired and gray-whiskered blacksmith in an old hat with holes burned in it by his forge. He appeared in an old gray military coat held together by a variety of buttons, only one a Confederate army button. Because of his comic uniform, he was promptly nicknamed, though not commissioned, "Major."

"Around the triumvirate—Dick Moran, John Underwood and Major Hibbs—," said Mosby, "recruits now gathered as iron filings cluster around a magnet."

The variety continued as the company grew. James F. Ames was a Yankee deserter. Unarmed but in full Federal uniform, he came to the Reb partisans from the Fifth New York Cavalry. A big man with slightly bowed legs, he walked with something of the swing of a sailor which he had been before the war. Mosby never discovered the grudge which prompted Ames' desertion. The leader never believed it was only, as Ames said, because of Lincoln's Emancipation Proclamation. Ames seemed to take a special pleasure in hitting his old Yank comrades. Some of the band distrusted Ames at first, but Mosby found him a valuable recruit. Desperately brave as he showed himself, he was soon affectionately called "Big Yankee" by all the men.

Others came. One recruit was a grinning Hungarian named Jake who had fought as a private under Kossuth in his homeland. A dark, romantic young Mississippian, Mountjoy, arrived. Then, with a letter from Stuart, Captain Bradford Smith Hoskins appeared in the neat uniform of an English officer who had fought in the Crimean War and under Garibaldi in Italy. He would have seemed more at home in Wyndham's company than in Mosby's tattered band. He thought riding with Mosby "better than a fox chase." Mosby's only fault with him was that "it was a point of honor with him to use his sword and not his pistol." That obsolete preference, John thought, later cost Hoskins his life. His other men, said Mosby, had "no more use for that antiquated weapon than a coat of mail."

No such scruples about arms attended a young Virginia divinity student, Samuel F. Chapman. As a militant Presbyterian, like Stonewall Jackson, he sang the Psalms of David as he galloped into battle. But he always exhausted every barrel of his two pistols before he went to work with his saber. He was, Mosby said, "generally in front of everybody in a fight." Mosby loved him as Robin Hood loved Friar Tuck.

"My men were not altogether of saintly character," Mosby said.

Not all of them were at first the most dependable soldiers. In one of his early raids two of Mosby's men, "Coonskin" Gall, named after the cap he wore, and one called Jimmie the Irishman, added comedy to the drama of war. When Mosby left them with a Union sympathizer whom he had impressed as guide, both tramped in a circle about a fire in the snow to keep warm. And suddenly each became suspicious of the other as a possible Yankee who had slipped up behind him. They began to shoot at each other. Fortunately in the shooting that followed only the guide was slightly wounded.

Mosby usually had less sympathy for such turncoats than for brave Yankees he fought. He enjoyed the discomfiture of another Southerner, who swore loyalty to the Union in hope of making money at his store. Not even the Federals trusted this man until after he had run for cover so fast, when Mosby fought near by, that he left the bung open on a barrel of molasses. The Yanks never doubted him after they saw his precious molasses shoe-deep on the floor of his store.

Some of Mosby's men trusted nobody. The leader put four captured officers on their parole, or oath, to report to Fitzhugh Lee at Culpeper and sent them with Jake the Hungarian as escort. As they went back Jake volunteered to shine their shoes every night. He came back grinning to tell the leader that by doing so he knew they would not slip off shoeless in the snow.

Around Mosby there was much hearty laughter as well as hoofbeats and gunshots in the dark. He wrote Pauline back at home with the children: "Have had a gay time with the Yankees." Also, as he captured men and took horses, he had some almost secret jokes of his own. He sent a veiled message back through General Stuart to Fitzhugh Lee who had demanded his men back. In terms of the increasing shortage of good horses in the Army of Northern Virginia, he wrote: "If you would let me have some of the dismounted men of the First Cavalry, I would undertake to mount them." Fitzhugh Lee was duller than Mosby thought him if he missed that barb.

Mosby's own men rode the best horses the United States Army could unwillingly provide. They poured out of nowhere, to hit Colonel Percy Wyndham's pickets everywhere. That Englishman had had enough humiliation from "horse thieves," he said. He put a column on the road with orders to catch Mosby and his motley band. Their sabers jangled against their spurs and the hooves of their horses resounded on the roads. John Mosby smiled from his hiding place.

"He might," he said of Wyndham, smiling wryly, "as well have been chasing the silver-footed antelope."

And while Wyndham's men burned the roads John quoted a couplet about the antelope.

> That gracefully and gayly springs
> As o'er the marble courts of kings.

Wyndham had less romantic ideas about the chase.

CHAPTER 6

Yankees in Pursuit

Though the proud and angry Colonel Wyndham called Mosby's men horse thieves, he was ready to use worse men to catch them. So, after dashing Confederate raiders went the so-called Independent Loudoun County Rangers. That organization was composed largely of native Virginians who were willing to serve the Yankees and, Mosby said, rob their neighbors at the same time. However, they had been commissioned as a Federal outfit, led by Captain Samuel C. Means, a businessman of the village of Watertown.

They hit Mosby's men not in a battle but at a dance. His men were no saints, as the Confederate ranger admitted. Some of his young fellows liked a frolic as well as a fight. They liked the music of fiddles as well as the crack of pistols. And loyal Southern girls welcomed their company. Mosby had ordered his men to meet him at Ball's Mill on Goose Creek, near the Loudoun-Fairfax County line, early on the morning of February 7, 1863. But the night before, while some were dancing at the house of a gentleman named Washington Vandeventer, fiddle music was interrupted by gunfire. Lamps were put out. A girl and two of Mosby's partisans were wounded. Four partisans were captured.

In the morning Mosby was almost more angry with his men than Wyndham was with him. Later he recognized that some good Southern cavalrymen joined him just to get a horse. Others, like members of undisciplined Highland clans, scattered after raids to go home with their plunder. He knew that discipline was essential if a small company was to succeed against greater numbers. Now he knew that no such raids as he had planned on the picket lines in Fairfax County, just across the river from Washington, could be made with the small number who answered his call. Nevertheless in that snowy February he began to get his revenge on the Yankee rangers whom he was ultimately to destroy. Their plan was to destroy him first.

The wiry Confederate's chance came quickly. Riding with his small force, he struck the trail of the Yank raiders. He met an old country physician, Dr. Drake, walking home through the snow and knee-deep mud. The Union riders had come upon him while he was visiting the sick. They had taken not only his horse but his saddlebags containing the drugs which could no longer be secured in the South.

"He told us," Mosby said, "that the marauders were not far ahead, and we spurred on to overtake them."

They found the Yank raiders where they had stopped to plunder a house. More intent to save their loot than to fight, the Federal raiders dashed away but were stopped by a swollen stream. Mosby took from them not only silver spoons they had stolen but good Dr. Drake's medical kit, too. He did not, however, catch all the Virginia raiders who were serving the Yankees. Some were waiting in ambush to catch him and others had another plan to put an end to his career.

As Mosby rode to strike at a Yankee picket post, a young lady hailed him in the road. She was Laura Ratcliffe. General Stuart had introduced John to her just before he let his young scout stay behind as a ranger. Now she told the partisan leader that a talkative Yankee lieutenant had told her of a plan to trap him. As a classics student the ruse reminded John of the wooden horse full of warriors the Greeks had sent into ancient Troy.

The turncoat rangers had sent a tempting train of wagons up the road in Mosby's direction, apparently without any guard.

"But in each wagon were concealed six of the Bucktails," said John of the Federal soldiers, "who would, no doubt, have stopped my career, if I had given them the chance."

He hit elsewhere and everywhere. He went on striking at pickets wherever he was least expected, sometimes in broad daylight to avoid the danger of ambuscades. His reputation spread, he said, as an almost mythological character "prowling around their camps in the daytime in the garb of a beggar or with a pilgrim's staff and leading cavalry raids upon them by night." Actually he fought always in his Confederate uniform. But panic often broke out in Union camps when he was nowhere near. Pickets became so nervous expecting his attacks that they fired at every noise. He robbed the Yanks of sleep, understanding that "no human being knows how sweet sleep is but a soldier." And sometimes very quietly he sent men like "Big Yankee" Ames to rob Yankee stables of horses without disturbing the Feds.

All the alarm bugles were set to blowing again, however, when on the cold, cloudy night of February 26, with twenty-seven men he roared down on a Federal cavalry outpost of a lieutenant and fifty men on the Ox Road in Fairfax County about two miles from Germantown. Quiet John Underwood led the way along a winding route through the forest. In the dark a light blinked through the trees. They could see a sentry walking his post. They went on for a quarter of a mile, then at 4 A.M., they halted and tied their horses.

Two men were to capture the guard while John and the others slipped to the rear for a surprise attack. Then suddenly, as all moved to carry out Mosby's whispered orders, the sentry fired and ran shouting to the log house in which his comrades slept. As if expecting the shot as a signal, Mosby and his men ran forward shouting and firing, too. Though armed with carbines and in a log house with shooting space where the chinking had been knocked out, the Yanks yielded quickly. A reserve of a hundred Federals half a mile away did not come to the rescue of their comrades. The Yankee lieutenant and three of his men were killed. Mosby carried off five prisoners and thirty-nine horses with all their equipment.

Colonel Wyndham was not alone in being furious. Across the river in Washington rumors spread that he and 800 of his cavalry had been captured. Washington newspapers demanded to know who was responsible for attacks right at the door of the Union capital. Wyndham's commander, young, handsome, self-indulgent Brigadier General Edwin H. Stoughton, was outraged. On March 1, Wyndham ordered Major Joseph Gilmer of the Eighteenth Pennsylvania Cavalry to take 200 men to march to Middleburg and exterminate Mosby's "gang."

Gilmer threw a cordon of pickets around the town. He personally searched the hotel, and apparently stopped several times at the bar. He took more and more courage out of a bottle. Still he found no Mosby. Then he ordered his soldiers to arrest every man they could find. All they could discover were old men but Gilmer mounted them, riding double behind his troopers, and carried them off.

Also John learned, as he wrote later with amusement, that there were a number of colored women whom Gilmer "invited or who asked to go with him. They had children,

but the Major was a good-natured man. So each woman
was mounted behind a trooper—and the trooper took her
baby in his arms. With such encumbrances, sabers and
pistols would be of little use, if an attack was made. When
they started, the column looked more like a procession of
Canterbury Pilgrims than cavalry."

There seemed nothing funny about the situation, however, when Mosby rode into town with seventeen men
after Gilmer had departed. Indignant ladies gathered about
him to tell him how badly the old men had been treated.
They told him how Gilmer had made even the most feeble
of them march in the cold street. The ladies wept at the
fate of their husbands and fathers. Mosby was properly
indignant.

"To avenge the wrongs of distressed damsels," said the
partisan leader who often laughed at romantic soldiers, "is
one of the vows of knighthood; so we spurred on to overtake the Federal cavalry, in hopes that by some accident of
war we might be able to liberate the prisoners."

Accidents of war, if they could be called that, were
available that day. Mosby first came on two cavalrymen
in the outskirts of the village. "They surrendered, of
course," he said, "and were sent to the rear." Then riding
ahead of five or six men, he came to the crest of a hill and
saw before him Federal cavalrymen whom he took to be
Gilmer's rear guard. Down toward them he went, suddenly discovering that he could not stop his spirited horse.
His charge was really a runaway. Fortunately for him the
Yanks were more surprised than he was. His horse galloped on straight through the bluecoats who had stopped
to feed their horses. Some of them took to the woods.
Others fled to a nearby mill, hiding in the hoppers where,
Mosby reported, they came near to being ground up into
flour. When the partisans pulled them out their blue coats

were white with dust.

Still not able to stop his horse, Mosby now ran helpless into another body of Yankees. They saw the stampede at the mill and Mosby, pistol in hand, rushing toward them. He jumped off his horse to save himself from capture but the Yankees without firing a shot wheeled and ran. Mosby's riderless horse clattered after them. John walked back to watch his men pulling dusty Yankee prisoners out of the mill. Then he discovered that these were not Gilmer's men but another body of Yankee cavalry.

If he was mixed up, however, so was Gilmer. That Yankee officer had continued to turn to the bottle to keep up his courage. And when the Yanks who had escaped the stampede at the mill came dashing behind him, he figured that they were Mosby's men trying to surround him. The Major fled at a speed which John could only describe by allusion to famous flights in literature.

"Even if he did think the force he saw was my command," the partisan declared, "it is hard to understand why he should run away from the very thing that he was in search of."

The Yankee Gilmer was not satisfied with the speed of his retreat. The ground was soft and his horses sank knee-deep in the mud at every jump. Some horses faltered and their riders fell by the wayside. Gilmer pressed on furiously. Then before he crossed the line into Fairfax County, with half his horses sticking in the mud, the befuddled Major abandoned the old men he had captured. The old fellows had to walk home. History does not record what happened to the Negro women and their babies. But poor Major Gilmer was convicted of cowardice and drunkenness. He never came after Mosby again.

At Middleburg, the partisan leader was weary but pleased. "At night," he recalled, "with song and dance, we celebrated the events, and forgot the dangers of the day."

Already, however, he had bolder plans in his mind. While he danced and sang with the ladies in Middleburg, he was probably more concerned about information he was receiving from another lady, pretty blond young Antonia Ford of Fairfax Court House. For her service to the Confederacy, General Stuart in a gay mood had made her his honorary aide-de-camp. Mosby had known her when he was quartered near her father's fine house while on picket duty during the first winter of the war. John, as always, was secretive about his undercover connections. But on March 5, three days after Mosby danced and sang at Middleburg, a Union soldier stationed at Fairfax Court House wrote a letter to a friend in Vermont. It read:

"General Stoughton, who commands the Second Vermont Brigade, has his headquarters in the village, although his brigade is five or six miles away. What he could or would do in case of an attack, I don't know, but it seems to me that a general should be with his men. If he is so fancy that he can't put up with them, the government had better put him out.

"There is a woman living in the town by the name of Ford, not married, who has been of great service to General Stuart in giving information et cetera—so much so that Stuart has conferred on her the rank of major in the Rebel army. She belongs to his staff. Why our people do not send her beyond the lines is another question. I understand that she and Stoughton are very intimate. If he gets picked up some night, he may thank her for it. Her father lives here, and is known to harbor and give all the aid he can to the Rebs, and this in the little hole of Fairfax, under the nose of the provost-marshal, who is always full of bad whisky. So things go, and it is all right. No wonder we don't get along faster."

When that letter was written Mosby had already sent his secret call to his scattered men. They were to meet on the evening of March 8, in the village of Dover, where, a little over two months before, Stuart had first agreed to let him stay behind as a ranger.

CHAPTER 7

Mounting the Stars

There was always welcome for the lean partisan leader at the home of such a Virginia gentleman as Lorman Chancellor. In Chancellor's pleasant brick house even the servants could be trusted. Mosby came early or late, always sure of a meal or a bed. He had been at Chancellor's when he first learned that Sir Percy Wyndham was coming after him. In Loudoun County, not far from Middleburg and the road south to Fauquier County and Warrenton, it was a good central place for his operations. So on March 8, he again had good food and pleasant talk at Mr. Chancellor's house. He showed excitement only as he was about to ride away.

"I shall mount the stars tonight," he suddenly told his host, "or sink lower than plummet ever sounded."

Then he wheeled off to the meeting with his men, remembering as he rode the motto, "Adventures to the adventurous." Before the night was over he was to have adventures which afterwards he could only describe with the help of a variety of literary and historical references. There seemed nothing bookish about him, however, as he reined up at his rendezvous with twenty-nine of his rangers. Tonight he was not waiting for Wyndham; he was going to get him.

His plans were not exactly new. Nearly a month before he had written Jeb Stuart that the cavalry on the Federal outposts around Washington could be captured. Now he wanted the Yank cavalry's British commander who had called him a horse thief. He had told his plans for the night to only Big Yankee Ames.

There was no longer any question in the minds of Mosby or any of his men about trusting Ames. The partisan leader said later that he never understood what Ames' motives were in deserting to him. And he added: "I never cared to inquire." He could trust him. Now Ames, with the secret of the ranger's mission, had been out scouting. It seems probable that in the week before this gathering of the band the Big Yankee had been in Fairfax Court House, looking around, asking quiet questions. Colonel Wyndham had his quarters there near the more elaborate ones of rich, sociable, young Brigadier General Stoughton, commander of the brigade defending the capital.

Certainly Ames had discovered that there was a break in the Yankee picket lines around Fairfax Court House. The gray-headed Underwood, who knew every path, led Mosby's men through the break across the melting snow and in the evening mist. A drizzling rain helped shelter them and once the picket line was passed without sign of a sentinel, Mosby felt that half of the game was won. It was not quite that simple. Mosby had planned to reach Fairfax Court House by midnight so as to get out of the Yankee lines by dawn. Some of his men got lost. His little column was broken in the dark. An hour passed while his band looked for each other.

After they closed up, they struck the highway between the village of Centreville and Fairfax Court House. Then two or three miles from the courthouse, they entered the woods to avoid the camps of Wyndham's cavalry. By the railroad station they slipped into the quiet town. In the pitch dark which hid the color of their uniforms, Mosby established his headquarters in the courthouse yard. All telegraph wires were cut. Sentinels were shown the business end of big revolvers. Mosby detailed squads to go to the stables and the officers' quarters. Ames and others were sent to get Wyndham for whom they had come. Big Yankee came back with some of Wyndham's officers but the bad news that the gentleman was safe in Washington.

Then as the squads gathered up prisoners and horses, Mosby learned that General Stoughton was sleeping at his headquarters in the two-story brick Gunnell house. And he was probably sleeping soundly, too, because he had had a big gay party earlier in the evening. Taking five or six men, the partisan leader galloped to the house. They dismounted and knocked loudly on the door.

"Who's there?" a voice demanded.

Mosby answered, "Fifth New York Cavalry with a dispatch for General Stoughton."

The door was opened by a lieutenant in his night clothes.

The chief raider grabbed the officer by his nightshirt, whispered his name in his ear, and demanded that he take them to Stoughton's room. The young officer looked at the barrel of the "remorseless revolver" as the raider called his gun. He obeyed. By a light which they quickly lit in the room to which the officer took them, they saw the General huddled in the covers, snoring loudly. Dispensing with ceremony, Mosby jerked off the bedclothes, pulled up the General's shirt and spanked him soundly on his bare behind.

"Get up, General, and come with me!" he ordered.

The Yankee commander sat up, outraged. "What is this? Do you know who I am, sir?"

Mosby grinned. "I reckon I do, General. Did you ever hear of Mosby?"

"Yes," said Stoughton eagerly. "Have you caught him?"

"No, but he has caught you."

The General glared. "What's this all about?"

"It means, General," said Mosby calmly, "that Stuart's cavalry have taken over Fairfax and General Jackson is at Centreville."

That was a big multiplication of Mosby's twenty-nine men, but it served.

"Is Fitz Lee here?"

The raider nodded.

"Then take me to him. I knew him at West Point."

Pleased as he was with his captive, Mosby was disgusted with him, too. He smelled of the wine he had drunk that evening. Mosby had heard that the young officer was a brave soldier, but a fop. Now with distaste he watched him dress. Later he could only describe this scene by referring to some of his strange book lore which always seemed odd in a two-gun ranger.

"He dressed before a looking glass," Mosby said, "as carefully as Sardanapalus did when he went into battle."

Probably none of Mosby's men had ever heard of that last, most effeminate and corrupt of the kings of Assyria. They knew what their leader expected, however. When he brought Stoughton down, the guards he had left at the door had all of the General's horses and couriers rounded up. At the courthouse meeting place the other squads were waiting. There were three times as many prisoners as raiders and each was mounted and leading another horse.

Now the great problem was how to escape with the spoils. As they were leaving town, an officer in a loud voice from a window demanded what the cavalry was doing in the street. The raiders laughed loudly and Mosby sent some of them to catch the man. They broke through the door but met there a lady fighting like a lioness. She was the wife of the shouting officer in the window, who turned out to be Colonel Robert Johnstone, the commander of the cavalry during Wyndham's absence. Mrs. Johnstone held the raiders off until her husband could run naked from the house to hide somewhere in the garden behind it. The laughing Rebs always insisted that he hid under a privy.

They did not have time to look long for the naked officer, wherever he was. Daybreak was coming on. Roosters began to crow as they reached the pike four miles from Centreville; they were fearful that Yankee cavalry would be coming after them. Then at Centreville they saw the campfires of other Federal troops. Fortunately their pickets had been withdrawn as dawn approached. They could see cannon bristling on the redoubts and a sentinel shouted to them to halt. Apparently, however, he concluded that they were a body of Yankee riders. Beyond the camps they came to a little stream called Cub Run. The stream was ordinarily easily fordable but the melting snow had turned it into a torrent. Still with the enemy in full view behind them, they had to go on. Mosby plunged in first and his horse swam to the other bank. Stoughton followed and came out shivering.

"Captain," he said, "this is the first rough treatment I have to complain of."

Mosby laughed and turned to more of his bookishness to express his feeling in terms of the poetry of Robert Burns.

"I knew that there was no danger behind us," he declared, "and that we were as safe as Tam O'Shanter thought he would be if he crossed the bridge of Doon ahead of the witches."

The whole population turned out to cheer them as they passed Warrenton. Across the Rappahannock, Mosby delivered his prisoners to the Confederate officer he most disliked, Fitzhugh Lee. As apparently the Yankee General had expected, Lee was very polite to him. Later Fitzhugh Lee even tried to have Stoughton quartered in a hotel in Richmond instead of a prison. But he treated Mosby with indifference. He did not ask the ranger leader to take a seat by the fire. What Mosby had done did not seem to impress Lee.

"The reception I received," Mosby declared, "convinced me that I was not a welcome person at those headquarters. So, bidding the prisoners good-by and bowing to Fitz Lee, I rode off in the rain to the telegraph office to send a report to Stuart."

He did not have to wait for Stuart to receive his wire. That great, gay General came into Culpeper that evening loud in his praise of John and his feat. John never forgot the joy Stuart showed when he met him at the railroad station. Stuart clearly felt that Mosby had mounted the stars. Yet Mosby had been hurt by Fitzhugh Lee's treatment of him. He was not as gracious as he ordinarily would have been about a commission as captain which Stuart brought from the Governor of Virginia. The ranger even questioned its validity since all Southern forces were now part of the Army of the Confederacy.

"I want no recognition," he told Stuart.

He meant, he said later, official recognition. He liked, he admitted, public praise as much as any other man. The generous Stuart understood his old scout's snappishness and quickly published a general order almost singing about Mosby's "boldness, skill and success, so signally displayed in his numerous forays upon the invaders of his native soil." He hailed the raider's "last brilliant exploit" as a "feat unparalleled in the war." Finally, the great cavalryman spread his praise to Mosby's "gallant band . . .worthy of such a leader."

John's resentment disappeared. He was not even troubled when, as he thought, Fitzhugh Lee tried again to deprive him of a command. Lee could never do that now. Perhaps Fitz Lee needed the men he tried to get back from Mosby. Certainly in the growing shortage of good horses in the Confederacy, he needed the Yankee mounts Mosby had brought. In that same month when Fitzhugh Lee fought brilliantly in a cavalry fight at Kelly's Ford on the Rappahannock, no one better than himself understood his disadvantage. Guarding Robert E. Lee's flank, Fitz Lee's brigade had 2,100 men on its rolls but for lack of horses he could mount only 800 sabers.

Before Mosby's rangers rode back to their raiding ground, their Captain presented General Stoughton's beautiful saddle to his beloved Stuart. Stuart sent his thanks and also a request about pretty Antonia Ford, who had been arrested as a spy after Mosby's Fairfax raid.

"I wish you would send me," said Stuart, "whatever evidence you may be able to furnish of Miss Ford's innocence of the charges of having guided you in your exploits at Fairfax so that I can insist upon her unconditional release."

Mosby was always glad to help damsels in distress, particularly damsels who had helped him. His evidence of the innocence of Antonia is not available. She was kept in the Old Capitol Prison for some months. Washington was pretty grim about Mosby and anybody who might help him. Apparently only the greatest Yankee saw any light side to his exploit at Fairfax. When President Lincoln was informed of the loss in the raid—a brigadier general and fifty-eight horses—the Union President shook his head.

"Well, I'm sorry for that," said Lincoln. "I can make new brigadier generals with a scratch of the pen, but I can't make horses."

And not all the Union's generals could keep Mosby's rangers from snatching the horses they had.

CHAPTER 8

Hunter and Hunted

A carriage, like that which John Mosby had escorted early in the war, carrying ladies to the rear for General Stuart, moved in Fauquier County in March, 1863. It contained a pretty woman and two lively children. Before and behind it rode troopers from Stuart's cavalry. Pauline Mosby was joining her now famous husband in the country where he was an eagerly hunted man.

The partisan leader had urged her to come before the Fairfax raid. When he carried Stoughton back, he had made arrangements with General Stuart for cavalrymen to escort her to the "very nice place about four miles from White Plains" which he had selected. It was a fine Virginia mansion which appealed to his pride for Pauline. Also the house, though secluded in a grove of large trees, was near a junction of roads along which Mosby might leave or arrive by several routes. The master of the house was James H. Hathaway. Erect and clear-eyed, he was too old to fight for Virginia but ready to take chances for the Southern cause. As the host of Mosby's wife he could be depended upon for the same courage and coolness which Pauline brought with her.

Captain Mosby did not slow down while he waited for his wife. Indeed, he wrote Stuart the same day, "I start with my command . . . to go down in the neighborhood of Dranesville." A large body of Yank cavalry was camped there. At Herndon Station on the Alexandria, Loudoun and Hampshire Railroad he surprised an outpost of over thirty cavalrymen lounging around a sawmill. In panic the Yanks fled to the second floor of the mill. They came out with their hands up quickly, however, when Mosby loudly shouted an order to set fire to the shavings and the sawdust about the mill. Near by, a few minutes later, Mosby also caught four Yankee officers who thought they were well-hidden in the attic of a Union sympathizer's house. When a ranger fired his pistol into the dark garret, however, a frightened major lost his balance on the beams on which he lay. Down he crashed through the plaster into the room below where the rangers waited. With their plunder and prisoners, the rangers spurred off just in time to escape a big galloping Yankee rescue troop.

A new hue and cry rose among the Yankees. Sir Percy Wyndham and General Stoughton no longer guarded the Washington defenses. Now President Lincoln put Major-General Julius Stahel in command of the cavalry there. Stahel had fought for freedom in Hungary. Before the war in America he had become a newspaperman. His appointment was hailed in jittery Washington. A newspaper which had reported Mosby's raids before it learned to spell his name declared that Stahel could be depended upon to watch "every movement of the small bands of guerrillas and other irregular troops that have alone perpetrated the mischief."

The capital was anxious for such watching. Above Mosby on the Potomac, it was said, the planks were removed from the bridges every night for fear the partisan leader might dash across. Perhaps even Lincoln did not take altogether as a joke the message a Northern woman brought him from Mosby. In Virginia the partisan leader had stopped a vehicle in which she rode. He treated her courteously but before he let her go on he clipped off a lock of his sandy hair. "Take this to Lincoln," he told her, "and tell him I'm coming to see him soon."

Such stories built the legend that Mosby was everywhere and might be anywhere. But bold Stahel meant to put up with the partisan's "mischief" no longer. Not only was it necessary that Washington be free from fear, but also Federal supply lines behind great Yankee armies along the Rappahannock were now more important. They had been reinforced, refreshed and rearmed after their defeat at Fredericksburg in December. The bad weather, which had turned the first Union efforts to strike back at Robert E. Lee into a "Mud March," was ending. Such a slap as Mosby had given at Herndon Station could not be tolerated or allowed to be repeated. Stahel stormed that order to his troops.

Yet at that very moment the "small bands" Washington feared were formally organized for more militant mischief. The Herndon Station raid brought praise from General Lee himself. The great Reb commander wrote Confederate President Jefferson Davis urging that Mosby be promoted to major, although his last promotion to captain had not yet arrived. And Jeb Stuart sent to his old scout Lee's instructions about organizing his band as a regular part of the Confederate Army. Stuart cautioned Mosby.

"By all means ignore the term 'Partisan Ranger,' " Stuart wrote him. "It is in bad repute. Call your command 'Mosby's Regulars.' "

Mosby calmly disregarded that advice. He did not want to be a "regular." Military formalities always bored him. He intended to be a free partisan. Also he declined to be hampered by the Confederate law which permitted the men to elect their officers. He had seen enough of that system when Grumble Jones was voted out for Fitzhugh Lee. The partisan leader, however, followed the letter of the law. He assembled his men.

"You will be known as the Forty-Third Battalion of Partisan Rangers," he told them. "It is my desire now to organize you who have gathered here as Company A of this unit. These are the men you are to ballot for as officers."

He read his ticket. There were no alternative candidates. "What is your will, men?"

As he intended and expected there was not a dissenting vote in the chorus of ayes. The command always rode under officers he nominated for them to "elect." It was growing but still small. On March 23, the same day on which his commission as Captain was belatedly made official in Richmond, the largest band he had ever led—sixty-five men—met him at Rector's Cross Roads. As he led them by the Little River turnpike, through the woods toward the village of Chantilly, Yank pickets gave warning. All chance of surprise was lost this time. Then from a camp of Stahel's cavalry, only two miles away, about a hundred Yanks galloped after the partisans.

From a hill Mosby saw them coming. He was ready to order a charge though he thought he had less than half their number, when he saw another troop of Yankees coming to reinforce the first. He ordered a slow retreat, keeping his men close together. The pursuing Yanks, he was sure, would string out along the turnpike and so lose their advantage in numbers. As the Rebs passed over a hill, they could hear behind them the loud cheers of the Union riders and the hoofbeats of their horses on the hard pike.

"I had either to suffer a stampede or make a fight," Mosby decided. "The cavalry officer who deliberates is lost."

Fortunately for him, a year before as a defense the Yanks had cut down some trees beside the road. Mosby formed his men behind them. Then as the Yanks came on he ordered his men to rush out with drawn sabers so as to give the impression that he had led the pursuers into an ambush. He had no faith in the sabers except for show. When fighting began he knew his men would use their guns. Now they charged out with a yell that startled and stunned the bluecoats leading the chase. Surprised, the Yanks faltered and halted.

"I knew then they had lost heart and were beaten," the partisan Captain said.

Before the Federal cavalrymen could wheel and run, Mosby's men were among them at work with their pistols. Routed, the pursuers quickly became the pursued. The partisans chased them for two or three miles. In the early dark, close to the Yankee camps Mosby halted them. His only casualty was a wound in the heel suffered by the almost maniac "Major" Hibbs who had fought with fearless joy. Many dead and wounded Yanks lay beside the road. The partisans carried off thirty-six prisoners and about fifty horses. They had beaten four times their number.

"Hurrah for Mosby!" cried General Lee when Stuart sent him the news. "I wish I had a hundred like him!"

In the country crowded with Federal cavalry, Mosby struck as if he were not merely one man but a hundred. His movements made some Yanks believe that Stuart's cavalry had arrived in Loudoun County. On March 30, with sixty-nine men, the partisan leader rode back toward Herndon Station. Finding there neither fight for his men nor forage for his horses, he moved northward along the Potomac.

At night the band found forage at the Miskel farm, north of Leesburg. It seemed a safe resting place though it lay in an angle between the impassable streams of the Potomac River and Goose Creek. The men put their horses in a field by the barn surrounded by a high board fence. The partisans went to sleep in the hay. But while they slept a Union woman sent word of their whereabouts to Major Charles F. Taggart, commanding the nearest Union cavalry post. Taggart sent 150 Yank cavalrymen under Captain Flint to catch Mosby and his men.

Fortunately the partisan chief had left the leather-lunged Dick Moran on guard on the Leesburg pike. At sunrise next morning Mosby was just pulling on his boots when Moran came dashing across the field.

"The Yankees are coming," he shouted.

Mosby rushed toward the fenced barnyard where the horses were. He had no time to saddle his own horse. Only about a third of the mounts of the partisans were bridled and saddled. The leader buckled on his pistols as he ran toward the yard. Then as the enemy poured through the farm gate, he directed the men not to fire but to saddle and mount quickly. As the Yanks came on, their sabers flashing in the morning sun, Mosby feared that his final hour had come. Still, as he saw the Union Captain divide his men so as to send some to the partisan rear, Mosby's hopes lifted.

"I had great faith in the efficacy of a charge," he said, "and in the affair at Chantilly had learned the superiority of the revolver over the saber."

On foot with pistols in hand, Mosby advanced to meet the Yankees coming through the gate. He called on his men to follow. They responded, yelling like demons. Harry Hatcher, one of the bravest, dismounted and gave Mosby his horse. On it he led the charge. Once again, expecting Mosby to take the defensive, the Yanks were surprised. As they faltered their captain was shot. Then they turned and tried to make the narrow gate through which they had entered. Packed and jammed there, the narrow passage became a bloody angle.

Mosby watched the fierce fighting of Hatcher on the horse of a Yankee he had killed. He saw one of his new men, the divinity student Sam Chapman, having exhausted every barrel of his two pistols, swinging with his saber. It did not seem an inferior weapon then. To give more power

to his swings Chapman was standing straight up in his stir-
rups dealing deadly blows from right to left. Yanks who
escaped the crowding at the gate fled down the pike. The
other cavalrymen who had been sent to the rear of the
partisans took panic at the sight. Mosby and his men followed in close pursuit almost to the Union cavalry camps.

Dead and wounded Federals were strewn along the road
from the farm to the end of the chase. The partisans'
losses were only one man killed and three slightly wounded.
At the end of the chase in Dranesville they had eighty-three
prisoners—more than the whole number of Mosby's band—
and ninety-five horses with all their equipment. And there
they found two sutlers' stores full of good things.

"These were, of course, appropriated," the Captain said,
"and helped to swell the joy of the partisans. A more
hilarious party never went to war or a wedding than my
men were returning home."

As they rode into Middleburg loudly singing, "The wine
cup is sparkling before us," there were so many blue-
coated prisoners among them that the citizens thought they
were a column of victorious Yankees. They were reas-
sured when the powerful, familiar voice of Dick Moran
shouted an "All right" that resounded through the little
town. The news quickly went to Jeb Stuart and to Robert
E. Lee, who was happy then to send on by special courier
Mosby's commission as Major, just two weeks after he had
been made a captain.

Along the Potomac General Stahel was not pleased. The
badly beaten Yankee cavalry, he said, had lost so good an
opportunity to catch Mosby that the result could only be
"ascribed to the bad management on the part of the officers
and the cowardice of the men." He promised to punish
those still living and uncaptured. Also, scorning inferiors,
he set out at the head of 2,500 men and four pieces of
artillery to do the Mosby-catching job himself.

He came pretty close to it once when Mosby had to slip through Stahel's men, with one companion, in the dark. Then the General marched and Mosby marched. A few partisans hit Stahel's advance-guard. They were gone when more Yanks came up. Often it was difficult to tell who was chasing and who running. From hilltops above the Yankee column the partisan chief in his plumed hat watched and mocked Stahel. On other hills other partisans looked down, dark figures against the sky. Mosby did not like Stahel. Using big words he called the Major-General a "whiskered pandour"—or a sort of Balkan country police-man. But he knew he could not meet and fight Stahel's whole force. And Stahel, not getting Mosby, took prisoner and carried off a group of old men like those the unfortu-nate Gilmer had arrested before.

No Yankee knew so well as Mosby, however, how near he came to being caught. Stahel not only marched the roads, he shelled some woods with artillery before he dared camp in them. Also he put guards all around the Hathaway house where Pauline was staying and where the Union commander hoped the ranger chief might come. Periodi-cally the bluecoats searched it. Time after time at night his officers rapped on the door of the big house among the trees. Lamp in hand, Old Man Hathaway always answered courteously and calmly. Pale and silent, Pauline watched as they searched for her husband. One night, if they had noticed, she must have been particularly pale. They went from room to room, searched every nook, cranny and closet. They looked under beds. Sharply they questioned Pauline and the old gentleman. Finally, though they had found a rumpled Confederate uniform, they gave up. Scowling and in bad humor, they left. Mr. Hathaway's hand trembled as he closed the door. Pauline ran up the stairs. Major Mosby swung himself into the window from the limb of the tree outside on which he had been calmly waiting for the search to end.

CHAPTER 9

High Price for a Gun

As spring came in Virginia the great armies of the North and South stirred above and below Mosby's little band. A larger and stronger Union army under General Joseph Hooker, who was called Fighting Joe, prepared to hit General Lee again along the Rappahannock. As Fighting Joe's supply lines became more important, General Stahel was even more anxious to protect them by catching Mosby. Not planning to be caught, the partisan chief set out to do as much damage as he could. General Jeb Stuart counted on his aid in interrupting Yank supplies and in reporting their movements.

"There is now a splendid opportunity to strike the enemy in the rear of Warrenton Junction," the great Southern cavalry leader wrote his old scout. "The trains are running regularly to that point. Capture a train and interrupt the operation of the railroad."

But, Stuart warned, "Keep far enough away from a brigade camp to get off your plunder and prisoners."

Mosby did not realize then how much he needed that warning. He was willing, he said, "to let the Union troops down in Halifax rest while I turned my attention to Joe Hooker." He slipped away from the Yanks whom General Stahel had fumbling on his trail and, on May 2, 1863, while the battle of Chancellorsville was raging, assembled his men. They moved swiftly and secretly toward the Orange and Alexandria Railroad. Mosby planned to go on to hit Hooker in the rear and burn his trains and rations while the battle raged. On the way, however, the partisans could not resist the chance of a good fight.

In sight of Warrenton Junction they found a body of Yank cavalry resting on the grass while their unbridled horses grazed. They were enjoying, Mosby said, the far-off music of the great battle and had no dream that danger was near. The partisans roared down on them, drove them into a house, so packed that it was impossible to fire into it without hitting somebody. Some surrendered quickly and others came rushing out when a fire was built about the house. Mosby had three times as many prisoners as he had men. Then, just as the Reb raiders were preparing to leave with the prisoners and the spoils, one of their band came riding up at full speed. A large body of Union cavalry was rapidly advancing. Mosby's lips tightened.

"Now we will whip them," Mosby said.

Luck did not always ride with him, however. This time before he could strike, the charging Yankees sent the greatly outnumbered partisans flying in every direction.

"It was a mistake my making this fight," Mosby admitted, "even if I had been completely successful. In all probability it saved Hooker's transportation. I learned wisdom from experience and after that always looked before I took a leap."

Even so, though he looked forlorn as he rode through Warrenton, he felt no discouragement. In a few days he burned two railroad bridges. Then far inside the enemy lines, he routed a Yank cavalry force which surprised him while he was resting and feeding his horses. This time again his faith in the pistol proved itself against the saber. Still, when superior forces came up, he held back from attack though knowledge of his presence kept the Federals nervous and alarmed and drew Union soldiers from the front. That was what Stuart and Lee wanted. It did not satisfy Mosby's men. They wanted prisoners, arms, horses and the good things in Yank supply wagons. So Mosby sent a message by the dependable Fount Beattie to Stuart.

"If you will let me have a mountain howitzer," the partisan told the General, "I think I could use it with great effect, especially on railroad trains."

Stuart sent a gun which had been captured from the Yankees. Mosby put the fighting divinity student, Sam Chapman, who had had artillery experience, in charge of it. With this little piece of artillery, on the night of May 29 in Prince William County, below Halifax, he camped with about forty men. Between Manassas and Catlett's Station along the Orange and Alexandria Railroad, they were so near the Union army that Yankee bugles woke them in the morning.

They slipped through the pines, cut the telegraph wires, and removed a rail from the track. The gun was mounted. Then hiding along the tracks they awaited a signal from a partisan sent to watch for the approach of the train. Chapman rammed down a charge in his gun. Mosby waited, fearful that the Yanks might be alarmed and stop the train.

Instead, down the tracks the engineer drove it at full speed. It hit the gap in the rails. Off the tracks it went, helpless and roaring. From the coaches blue-coated infantry guards fired a volley. Then Chapman's gun sent a shell crashing through the cars. Another shell blew up the engine's boiler. In the hissing steam the Yanks stampeded. The train was set afire. The United States mail bags were seized. And a whole car was emptied of sutler's stores, including some fine fresh shad, a luxury which the Rebs had not seen lately.

"The difficulty now was to get out," said Mosby. That was a quiet understatement. With the attack accomplished some of Mosby's men, "thinking they were going on a picnic," as he said, had slipped off to fry their shad and eat the other good things found. But the sound of the cannon

had given the alarm. In nearby Union camps bugles sounded the order "to horse." Mosby and his gunners galloped away. Suddenly when they were about a mile from the railroad, they met a regiment of New York cavalrymen. The partisan chief halted. Chapman unlimbered his gun again. He sent a shell which burst at the head of the Yank column. The Federals scattered and Mosby's men charged toward them. But other bluecoats were coming up. The partisans fell back to the gun and galloped with it down the road. The Yanks rallied and pursued.

Slowly withdrawing with less than fifty men, the partisan leader realized that he faced a whole Yankee cavalry brigade. In a hand-to-hand fight as they fell back, Captain Hoskins, the English officer, was killed. Mosby felt that Hoskins might not have fallen if he had fought with his pistol instead of using the sword in single combat in "the tradition of chivalry inherited from the ancient knights." As he died Mosby was beside him and described him in the Crusader's language he liked for such occasions—"as gallant a gentleman as ever pricked his steed over Palestine's plains."

The partisan leader rode on with two pistols in his hands. Then on a narrow lane between high fences he ordered a halt. Chapman loaded the howitzer with shot. Beside him stood Beattie and the handsome, brave Mississippian named Mountjoy. They had never looked so happy in their lives, Mosby said, though as for himself he wished he was somewhere else. As the Yanks galloped into sight Chapman sent a shell into their ranks and they fell back in confusion to the woods. Then foolishly, instead of spreading out, they came charging up the road in a solid column of fours. Chapman raked them with grape and canister. Bravely they charged again and again. Finally Chapman rammed home his last round of ammunition.

This time as the Yanks came Mosby ordered a charge. His spirited sorrel horse carried him through Union ranks.

But as he passed, a big Federal cavalryman with a saber struck him such a blow on his shoulder that he was nearly knocked off his horse. Mosby's pistol flamed and the Yank fell. Now the slim raider was hemmed in by the high fences. At last he reached the woods. A tree limb badly scratched his face. Behind him the Yanks had captured the gun. Mountjoy was captured and Chapman was badly wounded. Mosby escaped with a single companion.

"I stopped at a farmhouse," he said, "washed the blood from my face, and started back to get ready for another raid."

The Yankee cheers which he had heard as he fled, resounded in their camps. General Stahel wrote a dispatch about Mosby: "We whipped him like the devil, and took his artillery." But Jeb Stuart sent Mosby word that he would be glad to send him another gun if he could sell it for the price he had made the Yankees pay for this one.

Stuart had a right to be pleased. A little more than a week after this attack on the train, Stuart fought a tough battle at Brandy Station with the Yankee Cavalry General, Alfred Pleasanton. The Federal authorities held back 6,000 Yankee cavalrymen from that fight because, with Mosby around, they could not be spared from the defenses of Washington. Mosby's forty men and his little gun not only destroyed a train; also perhaps they saved the battle.

Mosby took no chances that the Yank cavalry would be removed from his heels. That is where he wanted them. Three days later he fought Yankee forces again, this time in familiar Fairfax County. There he captured prisoners and horses and prudently withdrew when a bigger force arrived. Day and night he worked at "my policy to keep up a state of alarm about the capital." That was more important than ever now. Lee's army in the high spirits which followed the victory at Chancellorsville was moving westward, then northward toward Pennsylvania. Fear of invasion grew in the North. And Mosby used what he sometimes called his "mite" to help increase the fears. On June 9, with his band now organized for better discipline under officers of his own choosing, Mosby crossed over the Potomac into Maryland.

His plan to cross at night failed when his guide lost his way. But at dawn his riders moved over the river at a ford near Seneca, less than twenty miles west of Washington, burned a boat on the Chesapeake and Ohio Canal, and defeated a larger force of Federals in a running battle. Then they dashed back across the river with seventeen prisoners, more than twenty horses and the flag of the Yank cavalry. John Mosby lost two brave officers on that raid but it had all the effect he desired in increasing alarm above the Potomac.

Now sure, though he had not been informed, that the Confederate army was moving north, he waited for Stuart who hailed his recent raid across the Potomac. On June 17, Major Mosby met the gay, gallant cavalry General at his headquarters near Middleburg in Fauquier County. As always after hard fighting, Stuart's men were merry with their commander leading them in song. The girls of Middleburg had come out of their houses, clapping and waving when Stuart's men appeared. At night they danced to the music of the General's own banjo player and country fiddlers. They sang lively and sentimental songs. One was about a girl left behind:

> The years creep slowly by, Lorena,
> The snow is on the grass again;
> The sun's low down the sky, Lorena,
> The frost gleams where the flowers have been.

Mosby himself looked as elegant as the plumed General.

One of Stuart's staff noted that he looked no longer like the slouching scout. The uniform he wore was immaculate from polished boots to the plume like Stuart's in his hat. He rode a prancing horse and brought as a present to Stuart, who was having more and more trouble getting horses, a beautiful spirited sorrel which had recently belonged to a Michigan officer. Mosby's men, however, were a rough-and-ready-looking lot. In good nature Stuart joked about them. They reminded him, he said, of a story about a coon hunter so frightening in appearance that the coon in the tree begged him not to shoot, came down and surrendered. He expected the Yankees would feel the same way. Mosby smiled.

Not all was gay in Stuart's camp, however. The General could get no accurate information about Hooker's army. One who saw him before Mosby arrived said that Stuart was silent, puzzled and doubtful, walking up and down, knitting his brows and reflecting. He greeted Mosby not only with gaiety but an exclamation of relief. Soon they were in private conversation. Then Mosby came out of Stuart's quarters. He mounted his quick gray mare and set out in a sudden, heavy storm for the Union camps down the hills further east. Stuart seemed more confident after Mosby set out to seek the information the General required.

CHAPTER 10

Gray Ghost and Gettysburg

Mosby had two plans as he galloped off from Stuart's quarters. He promised the General that he would soon have the information he needed about Hooker's movements. Also he knew that any strike he made east of the Blue Ridge would help General Lee marching toward Gettysburg in the Shenandoah Valley beyond the range.

At first the partisan leader headed his band toward Seneca on the Potomac where he had struck the week before. The day was hot and they rode slowly, stopping to rest at the house of a friendly farmer. Suddenly the sounds of guns off toward Aldie gave warning that Yanks were ahead. The plumed raider and his motley men could not reach the river without passing through Hooker's infantry. Mounting swiftly they rode to an elevation in the nearby Bull Run Mountains where they could see eastward clouds of dust rising on every road from Hooker's march toward the Potomac. Also, from some Yanks they captured, Mosby got more information which he sent back by a swift rider to Stuart.

Then cautiously he moved forward keeping himself and his band, he said, concealed "like Robin Hood and his merry men in the green wood until night." In the darkness and inside the Union lines, the partisans slipped close to the line of communications between the Union cavalry of General Pleasanton below Aldie and the main headquarters of the Federal army near Fairfax Court House. All around them were the noises and the fires of camps of Union soldiers. Along the Little River turnpike a continuous stream of bluecoats poured northward. With only three men Mosby left the cover of the woods and rode out into the column of Union troops as they passed along.

In the darkness their gray Confederate uniforms went unnoticed. They moved with the tide of troops until they came to a house where an orderly was holding by their bridles the horses of three officers. In response to Mosby's polite questions the unsuspecting soldier told him that they were the mounts of Union officers who had just come from Hooker's headquarters. Abruptly the partisan leader grabbed the man by his collar. He whispered into his ear.

"You are my prisoner. My name is Mosby."

At first the soldier misunderstood. He thought he was being called Mosby. Indignantly he denied it. He understood better when in the starlight he saw the gleam of a pistol. When the officers came out the partisan saluted them. As he stood by the very quiet orderly, they thought he was a Union officer. They told him they were carrying dispatches from Hooker to Pleasanton. Suddenly Mosby's companions showed them gleaming pistols, too. Mosby took the dispatches. By a flickering light he discovered that they contained just the information Stuart and Lee wanted. Scrawling a note to Stuart, Mosby sent the dispatches and the prisoners back to the General. With his two remaining companions the ranger chief lay down within a circle of Yankee campfires and slept soundly.

He was going to need the little sleep he could snatch in those days when a vast Union army crowded the area. And he could not be caught napping. Once he very nearly was. A Negro had carried word of his whereabouts to General George Meade, who was soon to succeed Hooker in command of the Union army. One night the "Gray Ghost," as Yankees had begun to call Mosby, and some of his men slept in a drenching rain on top of the Bull Run

Mountains. In the morning he rode out to discover a small body of Yank cavalry about a hundred yards away near a country church. Instantly he ordered a charge. The Federals fled, but as they dashed away a company of Union infantry in ambush behind the church poured a heavy fire into the partisans.

"Meade thought I was done for," Mosby reported, but that same day his band slipped into a supply train of twenty wagons and carried most of them off. More important, as a result of his raids inside the Union lines, Hooker recalled General Stahel to try again to catch the elusive ranger. Stahel had gone south toward Lee's army on the Rappahannock. He was about to make a very damaging attack on Confederate supply lines when he was ordered back. So Stahel said he was restrained from dealing "a fatal blow" to Lee's lines as the Southern General moved to invade the North. That was the kind of result Mosby sought.

Along with prisoners, horses and supplies, the Gray Ghost took back to Stuart a plan for General Jeb's part in Lee's invasion campaign. In his headquarters the Confederate Cavalry General asked "the fearless and indefatigable Major Mosby" for his opinion as to the best route for Stuart's cavalry to take into Maryland. The partisan knew all the roads. He knew the location of each corps in the Yankee army. He told Stuart they were wide apart. So he outlined to the General a plan as full of exciting possibilities as the famous ride around McClellan's army the year before. The gay cavalier cavalryman's eyes gleamed as Mosby outlined his plan. Perhaps the General did not have, as some of his critics said later, too great a love for bold raids. Certainly, however, Mosby's idea appealed to him that June when Confederate hopes were high.

The partisan leader urged Stuart to move through an unguarded gap he knew in the Bull Run Mountains. Beyond it, Stuart could cut his way right through the middle of the Union army and cross the Potomac at Seneca. That was the shortest route north, Mosby told him. Also it would give Stuart a chance to destroy Hooker's transportation as he went along and cut communication between the North and Washington. The danger in it was that Stuart as the eyes of Lee's army might be separated by the Union army from the Confederate Commander.

Stuart liked the plan. Lee, in an order which contained a lot of "ifs" about what Stuart could do, approved it. The Cavalry General issued final orders. Mosby was to cross the Bull Run Mountains again at night by a bridle path he had frequently used. Then he would meet Stuart near Gum Spring in Loudoun County and take command of the advance guard. General Lee, Stuart told the partisan, was afraid that Hooker might steal a march on him and get into Maryland first. Mosby was to check again whether any portion of Hooker's army was already crossing the river.

Before the partisan chief talked with Stuart he had already been continuously in the saddle for three days and nights, but he agreed to go back inside Hooker's lines. With just two companions he crossed the mountains that night and early the next morning was riding, with only a raincoat to cover his full Confederate uniform, through the Union army. Soon he sent one of his men back to Stuart with a dispatch that Hooker's army was not moving across the river. He captured four Union officers and sent them back by his other companion. Then having learned what he wanted to know about Hooker's force, he started back alone.

At least, he was alone at first. Then he took two Yankee prisoners. He tied the heads of the bluecoats' horses together to keep them from running away. Late in the afternoon they came to the pike below Aldie. There, blocking his way, was a wagon train more than a mile long, with a strong cavalry guard. Eager to get to Stuart that night, Mosby knew that if he waited for the train to pass it would be too dark for him to find the path over the mountains.

He took his pistol from its holster and held it under his raincoat. Cold-eyed he told his prisoners that if they spoke a single word they would be dead men. Then with them by his side he rode out into the pike among the Union cavalry. Still there was no chance to cross the road as a fence on the other side was too high for the horses to jump. So they jogged along with the Yank cavalry. Once Mosby's elbow struck a blue cavalryman as he passed him. At last they came to a side road and turned off. In the afternoon light the guarded train moved on. It was, however, too late to reach the mountains before night. He knew better than to sleep in the woods alone with his prisoners. So he let them go.

"Of course," he said, "I kept their horses. Early the next morning I was again at Stuart's headquarters."

At dawn on June 25, 1863, Stuart's column moved through Glasscock Gap in the Bull Run Mountains and toward Haymarket for its swing across Fairfax County to the Potomac. Mosby went by the same back ways he had been traveling to meet the General at Gum Spring. On the way he barely missed a second ambush prepared by General Meade. Then he realized that things were not going as planned. Hooker's army began to move toward the river. As the partisan chief hurried to join Stuart he heard the General's cannon. Stuart's dash had turned into a slugging fight.

Unexpectedly the Confederate cavalryman found the roads on which he meant to march crowded by Yankee forces moving toward the Potomac. Thousands of blue-coated men separated Mosby and Stuart. And Stuart was thrown two days off schedule in his Potomac crossing. That had a part in his failure to be at hand when Lee desperately needed him before Gettysburg. Some even blamed Stuart for the loss of the crucial battle. To the end of his days Mosby vigorously defended Stuart's course. Certainly Stuart never blamed Mosby.

When Mosby found he could not reach his General, he spent all day and night riding among the streams of Union soldiers. Recklessly, then hopelessly, he tried to find the Cavalry Commander. He took long chances. He hardly bothered to hide. Finally, he turned westward to the Shenandoah Valley and so made his way into Pennsylvania. Serving as he could as scout and ranger, he dashed into Hagerstown, Maryland, and for a few hours set himself up as its provost marshal. Then he went on as far as Mercersburg in Pennsylvania. There he learned of Lee's defeat.

Back in Virginia, he was quickly striking the Yankees again. Before the month of the great battle was over he was sending to Stuart at one time 140 prisoners and reporting the capture of "one hundred and twenty-five horses and mules, twelve wagons, fifty sets of fine harness, arms, etc., etc." His raids in Fairfax County extended as far as the outskirts of Alexandria on the Potomac south of Washington. To the delight of his men, in one raid he seized twenty-nine sutlers' wagons loaded with all the good food and special luxuries those army merchants sold to the Yanks. Mosby's men learned new tricks. Sometimes they crept into Union lines with cowbells around their necks to cover the sounds of their approach. Sometimes dressed as teamsters they slipped into the seats of the regular drivers of Yankee wagon trains. In the dark they drove the wagons to side roads where they could loot them.

Always they fought with the "remorseless revolvers." They took blows as well as gave them. On the morning of August 24, Mosby set out with his band to burn more Yankee railroad bridges. On the way, however, he caught sight of a large drove of fine horses being led along with an escort of fifty cavalrymen. Where such a prize was available bridge-burning could wait. A dozen more Union cavalrymen joined the guard but Mosby determined to attack.

He slipped up on the Yanks when they had dismounted to water their horses at a tavern. The partisans roared down upon them with a yell that scattered the frightened Federals in all directions. A few of the Yanks took cover and returned the fire. They were soon silenced. But when the rout seemed complete, as the partisan chief reported to Stuart, he was shot through the side and thigh. His men misunderstood his withdrawal and followed him. That gave some of the bluecoats time to escape to the woods. Otherwise, he said, the whole party would have been captured. As he reported it to Stuart that loss seemed worse than his wound. Still they carried off a hundred horses. And that night, at Mosby's direction, his men went back and burned a railroad bridge.

Mosby would not let his partisans stop just because he had a gunshot wound in his side.

CHAPTER 11

The Ghost and Grant

Rumors spread, in September 1863, that Mosby was dead. Then Northern newspapers stated that he had lost a leg. A woman came into Washington with the story that she had seen Mosby's rangers guarding him in a wagon on the road toward the Shenandoah Valley near Upperville. She said that "as he lay in the open wagon supported on pillows and shielded from the sun by umbrellas, his face had the ghastly hue of death upon it." There were reports that he led his dashing men while riding in a buggy.

Actually, less than a month after he was shot he was on his horse again. A week later he led his men all the way across Fairfax County to Alexandria and captured the chief aide to the Governor of the so-called "restored" Union State of Virginia. Also as the autumn turned the green woods red, he went to Richmond. There, beyond the great Union and Confederate armies warily watching each other, Mosby went to defend his band from attacks at home.

Among tired, hungry men in the regular Reb army there was jealousy of the partisans. Men who fought and marched under strict routine looked enviously at the partisans who fought and got plunder for themselves. Officers complained of men deserting the regular forces to join guerrilla bands. And critical attention was drawn to Mosby's men in the August in which he was wounded. Then newspapers reported that his men had sold at Charlottesville $30,000 worth of plunder they had taken from the Yanks. Even General Lee thought that Mosby's men were sometimes more intent on capturing sutlers' richly loaded wagons than hitting Union communications.

Mosby was in trouble. Some other bands of irregulars had behaved very badly indeed. But in Richmond he stated his case effectively. He wrote Pauline that he "went to see the Secretary of War, he spoke in the highest terms of the services of my command, said he read all my official reports. Also saw old General Lee, he was very kind to me and expressed the greatest satisfaction at the conduct of my command."

Lee did seem to be getting old as the grim winter of 1863-64 approached. His beard was gray. He was having more and more difficulty getting food for his men and forage for his horses. A stronger, magnificently equipped Union army was facing him across Northern Virginia. He did not need the constant glowing reports General Stuart sent him about Mosby's activities to realize the usefulness of the partisan band behind the Union lines. When the time came for him to decide about all the ranging bands, Lee recommended that Mosby's Forty-Third Battalion be retained. The slim major, he said, "has done excellent service, and from the reports of citizens and others I am inclined to believe that he is strict in discipline and a protection to the country in which he operates."

Mosby went back from Richmond to justify the faith shown in him. In reporting to Stuart, he wrote that "it would be too tedious to mention the various occasions on which we have met the enemy." Each was an occasion marked by dash, boldness and gunfire. The partisans dispersed like the children of the mist when a big body of Yanks thought they could trap them at Christmas. Then early in January, the Gray Ghost set out to attack the strategic Loudoun Heights above Harpers Ferry at the junction of the Potomac and Shenandoah rivers.

Perhaps Stuart suggested that. Certainly the General's

scout, Frank Stringfellow, brought Mosby information that the Union cavalry occupying the heights were a mile away from infantry support. So out of a terrific snowstorm, on January 9, 1864, one hundred and six men from three of Mosby's companies assembled at Upperville. That village is about twenty miles as the crow flies below Harpers Ferry. No crows were flying that night. Horses moved through foot-deep snow. As the band moved forward the snow stopped falling, but the night grew colder under the stars.

Counting on complete surprise, the partisan chief led his men by file along a narrow path up the heights. Once he had them there in a position between the cavalry camp and the Ferry, he was confident of success. No alarm had been given. The enemy slept. Quietly he sent Stringfellow and ten men ahead to capture the cavalry commander and his staff, who occupied a house about a hundred yards from their men. Mosby with the remainder of his men waited, pistols out and in hand.

Then suddenly Stringfellow and his men came back yelling and shooting. Mosby was amazed at them. He was disgusted with these men later. They had, he said, made no attempt to capture the Yank officers. Apparently they had become alarmed in the cold dark. Mosby, however, mistook the yelling men for the enemy. Quickly he ordered a charge. In the confusion, the Yanks were aroused. They greeted the partisans with a volley from their carbines. Still Mosby drove the bluecoats from their tents. They fled into nearby houses. But all element of surprise was gone.

In a few minutes Mosby knew Yank reinforcements would be coming from the infantry camps nearby. Shrilly, he called for retreat. Some partisans did not hear him. Others were down, badly wounded. Still the band got away with six prisoners and between fifty and sixty horses.

More baffling to the Yanks who galloped in pursuit, the tracks of the partisans in the snow ended a little way up the Shenandoah River. There they led to the edge of the water. But nowhere along the banks were any tracks where they left the stream. Along the high-cliffed shores of the Potomac and the Shenandoah, legends grew about caves through which riders could escape and secret ravines where horses could be hidden.

"My loss was severe," Mosby reported frankly, "more so in the worth than the number of the slain."

One was Captain William R. Smith, the senior of his company captains. Another was Lieutenant William Turner, one of the original rangers. Other brave men were lost. Nevertheless General Stuart, when he received the partisan chief's report of his defeat, passed it on with undiminished praise. Mosby's exploits, the General said, were not surpassed in such fighting in any age. He urged the Major's promotion. And on February 11, Stuart happily sent a note to Pauline as "Mrs. Lieutenant Colonel Mosby" announcing that Richmond authorities also thought the Gray Ghost deserved a higher rank.

Stuart sent his merry message to Pauline at the house of Joe Blackwell near Piedmont. The Hathaway house at White Plains had been searched too regularly to serve any longer as Mosby's headquarters. And the Blackwell house would soon be spotted and burned. Still Stuart never failed to know where he could reach the elusive partisan leader. He sent to him not only praise but brave men from all over the world who came seeking a good fight. Baron von Massow, then a young Prussian lieutenant, who later became chief of cavalry in the Imperial German Army, arrived. He fought with the Gray Ghost in another raid at Dranesville late in February. There, at the cost of a serious wound, the German learned with Mosby the superiority of the pistol over the saber.

Yanks were learning the new tricks of the fighting trade, too. Early in the war the Southerners had seemed to have greater natural ability as cavalrymen than the Northerners. Hunting and horse-racing had long been favorite pastimes in the South. The mounted man was the symbol of the romantic notions of its chivalry. But many of its bravest riders, some of them foolhardy in the chase, had been killed. The supply of good horses in the South had almost been exhausted. And in mounts and men Yankee cavalry had steadily improved.

The Federals were ready to use any possible means to catch Mosby. They offered bribes to informants and some spies and traitors tried to collect the money. Once General Pleasanton made the ridiculous suggestion that Mosby himself might be bribed to betray the South. His superiors told that General to go the limit if he could: "do not hesitate as to the matter of money." The Gray Ghost only learned of this after the war. Then he laughed at Pleasanton's folly but he was pleased by the unlimited price the North put on him.

The Yanks gave him plenty of cold steel, however. As the war moved into its last year they put better soldiers before him. One was Colonel H. M. Lazelle, an old Indian fighter who proposed to use the methods he had learned against the redskins on the plains. Another was William S. Forbes, "the fighting major" of the Thirteenth New York Cavalry. Mosby bested both, though after he captured Major Forbes in a fierce battle at Mount Zion Church, he and the Yankee major became lifelong friends.

Bigger enemies were coming to catch the rangers. Out of the West came diminutive, hard-riding General Philip H. Sheridan. He brought with him a dashing, blustering lieutenant, George A. Custer, who rode with his long, golden hair flying behind him. Both came as the cavalry chiefs of a small, black-bearded man who seemed always to be chewing a stubby cigar. The North expected him to hammer Lee's already battered army into final submission. His name was Ulysses S. Grant. And only luck saved him from Mosby before he had a chance to strike at Lee.

During March and April 1864, the Gray Ghost found few good opportunities for successful attacks on the Federals. Suffering under the hard blows he had hit them in the winter, the Union commanders put out stronger outposts and showed great vigilance. Furthermore, as the Confederate army on the Rapidan and Rappahannock expected another big Union assault, General Stuart asked Mosby's help in scouting the enemy's gathering forces both east and west of the Blue Ridge.

Mosby was not one to miss a chance to attack, however. Early in May as the partisans watched the movement of Federal troops southward toward the impending battle of the armies, the Reb ranger saw his chance. Late in the day near Centreville, west of the Orange and Alexandria Railroad, he found a small group of blue cavalry. The very appearance of Mosby's band frightened the Federals. On the warm spring day the roads were dry again. Putting spurs to their horses the Yanks set up a cloud of dust as they fled, with Mosby's shouting men behind them.

Straight toward the railroad they ran. The flying Federals jumped the tracks at Warrenton Junction. The partisans followed furiously. In doing so the Rebs left a greater catch behind them. Down the tracks a train chugged toward the ruins of the station Mosby and his men had burned a year before. On the train, unknown to the Gray Ghost, was the high command of the Union Armies on its way to the opening of the great Battle of the Wilderness. General Grant was aboard. So was General Custer who was to cause Mosby anger and trouble—and get both in return. General Grant told the story in his *Memoirs*.

"On my return to the field on this occasion," he wrote,

"as the train approached Warrenton Junction, a heavy cloud of dust was seen to the east of the road as if made by a body of cavalry on a charge. Arriving at the junction the train was stopped and inquiries made as to the cause of the dust. There was but one man at the station, and he informed us that Mosby had crossed a few minutes before at full speed in pursuit of Federal cavalry."

Grant then, ready to lead the final great drive on Richmond, commented on the incident afterwards.

"Had he seen our train coming," he said, "no doubt he would have let his prisoners escape to capture the train. I was on a special train, if I remember correctly, without any guard."

Certainly if Mosby had known, he would have quickly made a Stoughton out of the Commander-in-Chief of all the Union Armies.

CHAPTER 12

Measure for Measure

If Mosby did not catch Grant's train, he followed the General southward to attack his communications along the north bank of the Rappahannock. At the same time he sent others of his growing band to harass the army of General Franz Sigel in the Shenandoah Valley. Then on May 10, 1864, he was back with all his band in the Shenandoah Valley at Front Royal. He hit some Yanks hard there that day. He was in that neighborhood when his faith in the invulnerability of any man received its hardest blow.

Almost unbelievably, on May 12, Jeb Stuart was dead. Grant's hard rider Phil Sheridan had roared toward Richmond with 12,000 sabers. And Stuart with all the cavalry he could muster, 4,500 men on worn-out horses, turned the Yankees from the straight road to Richmond. But in that fight at Yellow Tavern, Mosby's beloved General, who had never been touched by a bullet or a saber, was shot at close range by a dismounted Federal cavalryman. Also the news came that Mosby's first captain, Grumble Jones, cursing above the noise of a battle in the Shenandoah Valley, had fallen as he fought. Then in mid-June Lee's army, despite the slaughter of brave Federal troops at Cold Harbor, was locked in the final siege of Petersburg. Mosby rode and fought harder. The little village of Salem, high on a ridge fifteen miles northwest of Warrenton, became the center of his operations. Between the Bull Run and the Blue Ridge mountains at the center of Mosby's Confederacy, roads crossed there leading in all directions. From it he raided wagon trains, tore up railroad tracks and hit detached groups of Yanks wherever he could catch them. Early in July he moved to help the Confederate General Jubal A. Early. Lee had sent Early into the Valley to strike at Maryland and Washington. The Confederate Commander hoped that would frighten the Federal Government, as similar strikes had done before, into recalling some of the Yankee forces before Petersburg. Early roared down the Valley and Mosby's men hurried to his aid.

Once again the rangers slipped across the Potomac at Point of Rocks. They drove out the Yank garrison of 250 men there. Then they cut the telegraph wires. Washington could not find out what Early was doing, but panic spread in the reports that he was moving on Washington. Early reached Washington and even, for the only time in American history, had an American President under fire, when Lincoln watched the fighting at Silver Spring. Grant's rescue force was too strong for Early, however. He retreated. So did Mosby but with cattle and wagons, horses and prisoners. And Mosby celebrated his own recrossing of the river by routing a body of New York and Massachusetts cavalry at Mount Zion Church. The Federal force thought it had an excellent chance there to "whip Mosby."

"The chance was lost," said a Union officer in his report of the fight.

The chance was generally lost when Mosby was fighting. Now Grant, hammering Lee at Petersburg, determined to end the foolishness in Northern Virginia and the Shenandoah Valley. He sent the confident Sheridan to defeat Early and to clean the country of Mosby's "guerrillas." Facing this greater force, the Gray Ghost understood his job. He sent some of his men to attack all along Sheridan's lines west of the Blue Ridge. Others continued raids on the defenses of Washington in Fairfax and Loudoun Counties. From his mountain hideout he kept up alarm on both sides of the mountains.

Sheridan took formal command of the Army of the Shenandoah on August 7. Within the week Mosby hit him hard. One of the Gray Ghost's scouts learned that a 525-wagon train of supplies was moving down the pike to Sheridan. It was strongly guarded. Still the partisan chief set out with 250 men and two howitzers. After sundown on August 12, the band crossed the Blue Ridge through Snicker's Gap. They waited at Berryville near the Shenandoah River. Then in the dawn Mosby mounted a gun on a knoll beside the pike.

His men were obscured by the mist. But a comic situation almost defeated them at the start. The gun had been mounted over a nest of yellow jackets and the angry insects almost routed the Rebs before the Yanks could get a chance. Quickly, however, a partisan risked the yellow jackets and a shell roared like a clap of thunder into the wagon train. A mule's head was shot off. And down upon the startled Yanks charged the rangers. Panic spread among the Federals. Rangers went to work unhitching mules, burning wagons and hurrying prisoners and spoils to the rear.

Mosby deployed some of his men to give the impression that he had a larger force while others took between 500 and 600 horses, 200 beef cattle, and 200 prisoners over the Shenandoah River and away. Mosby lost only two men killed and three wounded. But in one of the wagons he burned up—"this we did not know at the time"—was $125,-000 in paymaster's cash. That was a loss Mosby's men did not care to remember.

Sheridan was furious. Above him Grant seemed even angrier. They talked of burning and hanging. So began the campaign to lay waste the Valley, to destroy the wheat and hay, to seize all the horses, mules and cattle. In Sheridan's words the plan was to make the rich, green Valley such a desert that a crow flying over it would have to carry its own rations. And while his men burned and destroyed, Sheridan with 56,764 men against Early's 12,509 pressed hard up the Valley. On September 19, the Yankee general routed Early in the Battle of Winchester.

Mosby was not riding then. Four days earlier, on September 14, while scouting in Fairfax County, he and two of his rangers met five enemy cavalrymen. Yanks and partisans all fired at the same time. Two of the Federals' horses were killed, pinning their riders under their bodies. The other three fled. But one of the Yank bullets had struck the handle of Mosby's pistol and glanced off into his groin. As quickly and as secretly as they could, Mosby's men carried him to his father's house in McIvors, a village near Lynchburg, behind the Confederate lines. He left in command in his absence the fighting divinity student, Sam Chapman.

The rangers fought well while Mosby was gone. Chapman routed a Federal force sent out to look for the wounded chief. His men struck at outposts in Fairfax County. They carried on harassment of the Federals trying to rebuild a railroad westward from Manassas Junction. Unfortunately, however, on September 22, Chapman undertook an attack on a wagon train rolling toward Front Royal with an escort apparently composed of about 200 men. He divided his men to attack at front and rear. Suddenly at the time he had ordered the attack, he discovered that the train was not only attended by 200 men but by a whole brigade of cavalry. The partisans were routed. Six were captured.

Then the golden-haired General Custer rode up. Earlier partisan attacks had brought his anger to the boiling point. Now he believed a story that a Federal lieutenant who had been killed in the fight had been shot after he surrendered. Custer ordered the six captured partisans executed. Into Front Royal the prisoners were led while a Yankee band played the dead march. Two were shot in a churchyard. Another was shot along the road. Then a seventeen-year-old boy who had just joined the partisans that day was killed before his mother's eyes.

With more music the Yanks carried two other rangers to a field between the town and the Shenandoah River. Custer, in a splendid suit of silk velvet, looked on as nooses were adjusted about their necks. With their hands tied behind them, the two partisans were placed on horses under a tree to which the ropes about their necks were tied. The younger of the two was crying. But the older ranger, a black-haired Georgian, sat erect. And just before the horses were whipped from beneath them, he shouted his defiance.

"Mosby'll hang ten of you for every one of us," he cried.

When the partisans later crept to the field to find the bodies of their friends, they also found around their necks crudely lettered signs: "This will be the fate of Mosby and all his men."

The Yanks were getting tough. Things looked dark, too, in Richmond and Petersburg when Mosby, able to travel only in an ambulance, went there during his brief convalescence.

"Colonel," General Lee told him there, "the only fault I have ever had to find with you is that you are always getting wounded."

But Lee had more work for him. General Grant was hoping that Sheridan could clean out the Shenandoah Valley and join him for a final assault on Lee before winter came. The Confederate Commander counted heavily on the attacks of the partisans on Sheridan's rear to delay Sheridan. So, lean and pale, still on crutches and wearing a scant sandy beard, Mosby joined his band. The partisan chief showed his anger when his men told him of Custer's execution of their comrades. He did not disclose his plans of retaliation. Sheridan quickly knew, however, that he was back.

Night after night and in broad daylight, too, the partisans roared down on Sheridan's men who were trying to build the railroad west from Manassas. Outposts were captured, trains derailed, and Yanks chased off with their guns and tools. The work had to be stopped and the line abandoned. The Yankee cavalry chief was even having trouble getting dispatches through to Washington. Then, where he was least expected, Mosby hit his hardest blow on October 13, 1864.

The Gray Ghost had been hurt again. His mount had been shot in a fight. As Mosby stood, dismounted, a Yankee cavalryman's horse trod on his foot. Now he rode wearing one boot. His other foot was so bruised that he could wear only a sock on it. He had to use a cane when he walked. Just two weeks, however, after he had returned, he pressed his men north and west across the Blue Ridge and the Shenandoah River. After riding all day they came to the line of the Baltimore and Ohio Railroad between Harpers Ferry and Martinsburg.

On the bright, clear night, with frost white upon the ground, they waited near the village of Kearneysville for the westbound passenger express. In a cut through which the tracks ran, they removed a rail and then, tired out, went sound asleep. They were almost as surprised as the train's passengers were when the roaring express jumped the track and its boiler exploded. Above the hiss of steam came the screams of passengers—especially women. The partisans were not long stunned. Mosby sent them hurrying down the bank to pull out the passengers and burn the cars. One car was filled with German immigrants who had bought tickets to the West and refused to move.

"Set fire to the car and burn the Dutch if they won't come out," Mosby ordered. When his men piled bundles of newspapers on their way to Sheridan's army and set them afire, the Germans hurried out. The partisans ran through the train collecting spoils. They were interrupted momentarily by a false alarm that Yankee cavalry was coming. The report came, Mosby learned, from one of the pickets he had put out who could not bear to be at a distance when his comrades were having such rich pickings. The spoils were rich. Two Federal paymasters were found with satchels full of Union greenbacks, as paper money then was called.

"Whether my men got anything in the shape of pocketbooks, watches or other valuable articles," Mosby said slyly, "I never inquired."

He was amused, however, by the case of a young German lieutenant who was on his way to serve in Sheridan's army. The young man was dressed in a fine beaver-cloth overcoat, gleaming boots and a new hat with a gilt cord and tassel.

"We have done you no harm," Mosby said to him. "Why did you come over here to fight us?"

"Oh," the German said. "I only come to learn de art of war."

A little later Mosby saw him again. Much changed in appearance, he came rushing to the Gray Ghost complaining. One of the partisans had made him swap fine clothes for old ragged ones.

"Didn't you tell me you came to Virginia to learn the art of war?" the Gray Ghost asked.

"Yes," said the unhappy German.

"This," said Mosby with his thin smile, "is your first lesson."

As the train burned the dawn was coming on. The partisans mounted. They crossed the Shenandoah and the Blue Ridge again. Next day, safe in a Loudoun County hiding place, the satchels of greenbacks were opened and distributed with no distinction between the eighty-four officers and men engaged in the raid. The bags contained $173,000. With part of it the men bought uniforms which made each of them as elegant as the German lieutenant had been before he lost his clothes.

Mosby would take none of the money, despite the insistence of the men that he share in it. So they made up a purse and bought for him a beautiful thoroughbred horse, named "Croquette," which he had seen and admired in a pasture at Oatlands, the beautiful Carter estate in Loudoun County. Croquette was to be his favorite mount. But the Gray Ghost had something more on his mind than horses or money. He had not forgotten Custer's execution of his men.

He acted slowly and reluctantly. First he secured the approval of General Lee. Then on November 6, the Gray Ghost lined up twenty-seven Yankee prisoners of 700 whom he had taken since Custer hanged his men. Seven of them drew marked slips. But one was a drummer boy. Mosby ordered that another be drawn to fill his place. The he sent the seven under guard to a point as close to Custer's headquarters on the Valley turnpike as they could be safely taken. Two of the Yanks escaped. Three were hanged at Berryville. Two were shot. On the body of one of those hanged, a sign was placed: "These men have been hung in retailiation for an equal number of Colonel Mosby's men, hung by order of General Custer at Front Royal. Measure for measure."

Then through the lines, under a flag of truce, he sent a scout to Sheridan at Winchester. The Reb carried a letter to the Yankee general. After reciting the facts, Mosby concluded:

"Hereafter any prisoners falling into my hands will be treated with the kindness due to their condition, unless some new act of barbarity shall compel me reluctantly to adopt a line of policy repugnant to humanity.

"Very respectfully, your obedient servant,

"John S. Mosby."

General Sheridan understood. No further "acts of brutality" were committed on Mosby's men.

CHAPTER 13

A Wedding and a Wound

"I will soon commence work on Mosby," Sheridan informed the War Department in Washington.

Exaggerating a little, the Union General said in November that he had so far made no attempt to break up the partisans because it would take ten men to Mosby's one to do so. Now he proposed to put fire to Loudoun County and thus create "an intense hatred of him in that portion of the Valley which is nearly a desert." His men came over the Blue Ridge, applying torches to haystacks and barns, burning fields and smokehouses, killing or driving off the livestock. But they never found Mosby, and the hatred Sheridan created was directed by the people not at Mosby but at himself.

Indeed, by December 1864, the Gray Ghost was the only defender Confederates had in Northern Virginia. In a series of battles Sheridan had defeated Jubal A. Early's men. What was left of them had been transferred to Lee's thin lines about Petersburg. Still Mosby's few hundred rangers kept Sheridan's soldiers as busy as when Early's army confronted them. The Yankees' scorched-earth policy had only made the partisans more furious in their attacks. They went into no winter quarters. In snow, sleet and howling storms—"in the long watches of the winter nights," as Mosby himself put it—Sheridan's men were kept in fearfulness that a sleepless enemy would capture or kill them.

Mosby's importance was never greater in the desperate

South than when he went to Richmond again on December 5. Newspapers noted his presence. He talked with General Lee about extending his operations. While there he was promoted to the rank of full colonel. The War Department gave him permission to organize his command into two battalions. At a frugal dinner, the Confederate Commander proposed to Mosby that in addition to his operations in Loudoun and Fairfax counties, he send some of his men to the Northern Neck in eastern Virginia.

Back with his band, Mosby put the reorganization of his growing force into effect immediately. He was in high spirits. Also, as he reported himself, he was better dressed that day than he had ever been during the war. Just before starting to Richmond he had secured through the blockade across the Potomac a complete new uniform. Now he wore a drab hat with an ostrich plume and a gold cord and star. With his gray sack coat bearing the insignia of his rank, he had on gray trousers with a yellow cord down the seams and long bright cavalry boots. Attached to his heavy, black beaver-cloth overcoat was a cape lined with English scarlet cloth. He was dressed for his new eminence—and for a wedding.

War did not stop romance. And that night the Gray Ghost's ordinance sergeant, Jake Lavender, was to marry a pretty girl named Catherine Edmonds. The ceremony would not be complete without Mosby's presence. With one of his rangers, Tom Love, he rode to the Blackwell house where the wedding was to take place. In the midst of the wedding festivities, however, a report came that Yankee cavalry was near by. Mosby did not want to break up the party, so with only one man, Tom Love, he went to investigate.

They met the Yankees but escaped to a hilltop where they watched the cavalrymen going into camp for the night. Mosby planned to attack them in the morning. He and Love rode to spread the call to other rangers. A drizzling rain was falling and freezing. Icicles hung from the trees. The two men were cold and hungry when they saw the bright windows of a Virginia gentleman, Ludwell Lake, who was famous for the good food he still managed to serve in the devastated region. Cheated of his wedding supper, Mosby decided to go in. Love said he would wait and watch the horses.

"No, Tom," Mosby said, "it wouldn't do me any good if you were to stay out here in the cold. There is no danger. Get down."

Soon they were having a fine supper with the Lakes and a friend, Mrs. Landonia Skinner. Then suddenly they heard the tramp of horses around the house. Quickly Mosby opened a door of the dining room toward the back yard. Yankee cavalrymen were there. Hardly had he slammed the door, however, before other Yankee officers and soldiers entered at the front. Mosby put his hands on his coat collar to conceal his rank.

Quickly firing began in the back yard. One of the bullets passed through the window. It made a round hole in the glass and hit the Gray Ghost in the stomach.

"I am shot!" he shouted.

Afterwards he said that the wound did not hurt much then but that he cried out to create confusion. He succeeded. As the firing continued those in the room rushed about. The supper table was knocked over. The tallow lights went out. In that moment of confused darkness, with 300 Yankees around the house, Mosby realized that his only chance was to play the part of a dying man. That did not require much acting. He was terribly wounded. He was bleeding profusely and beginning to feel faint. Still he hurried through a door into an adjoining bedroom. There he pulled off his coat bearing the insignia of his rank and tucked it under a bureau so that no one could see it.

He lay down with his head toward the bureau.

Behind him in the dining room old man Lake and the women were screaming. The Yankees quieted them. The Gray Ghost heard the Federal officers questioning Mrs. Skinner. Fearfully he waited for her answers. The wounded man was a stranger, she told them, not one of Mosby's men, and she did not know his name. Then the Yankee officers came with a candle into the bedroom to look at the partisan chief. He gave them a fictitious name and regiment. The Federals pulled up his blood-soaked flannel shirt and looked at his wound. Mosby gasped for breath. A Union doctor examined him, too, and pronounced the wound a fatal shot through the heart. Then stripping Mosby of his boots and trousers, and taking his hat and overcoat, the Yankees hurried away. Only one Irish bluecoat seemed doubtful.

"He is worth several dead men yet," he said.

There was a good deal of whisky on the breath of his examiners, Mosby said later. At the time he lay listening as the Federals left. When he was sure they were gone, he rose in a pool of blood and stumbled into the dining room. His friends there were amazed to see him. They examined the wound before the fire and all still feared it was fatal. Nevertheless, Lake got two Negro boys to hitch up a pair of young, half-broken oxen. Mosby was wrapped in blankets and put in the ox-cart to get him away for fear the Yankees might come back. He was stiff with cold when, through the sleet storm, he arrived at the house of another friend a few miles away.

A courier was hurried away to the wedding party. Before daybreak the partisans assembled again, this time around their apparently dying chief. Two surgeons came with them. One of the men present had been with General Stuart when he was killed a few months before.

"Look at my wound," Mosby asked him, "I think I am

shot just like General Stuart was."

Early in the morning the bullet was extracted. It had not gone through the Gray Ghost's body but only penetrated the surface. A week later, by back ways and guarded by partisans ready to be fiercer than they had ever been in a fight before, Mosby was carried again to his father's house near Lynchburg. That was a dangerous ride. Already the Yankees had learned that they had let Mosby slip through their hands again. Indeed, the suspicious Yankees showed Mosby's hat and overcoat which they had carried off from the Lake house to Reb prisoners, including Mosby's companion, Tom Love. All of them said solemnly that they had never seen them before.

A week after he was wounded, however, the Yankees knew that they had missed the man they wanted most. Federal cavalry tracked him to Piedmont, then to Salem, and out of Salem toward the Warrenton pike. They discovered that partisans had been strung out along the roads signaling as Mosby's ambulance moved along. Still Sheridan was sure on the last day of the year that Mosby had died of his wound in Charlottesville. On the same day, however, *The New York Herald* was not so sure.

"If we are to believe the Rebel stories," that staunch Union paper said, "Mosby is not yet dead. He may possibly recover: 'The devil takes care of his own.' "

Far from dead, though pale and thin, the Gray Ghost was greeted with cheers when he appeared in the halls of the Confederate Congress in Richmond on January 30, 1865. There was not much to cheer about in the Confederate capital then. Eager for something to applaud, a Richmond newspaper observed that "South Carolina, in the first revolution, was justly proud of her Marion . . . and Virginia today is no less proud of her fortunate son whom the Yankees denominate a guerrilla and a bandit."

General Lee welcomed him at his headquarters in Petersburg where the Confederate Commander was sharing the starvation rations of ragged troops. Mosby's practiced eye did not miss the bony horses hardly able to pull the Reb guns. The last Confederate seaport had fallen. General William T. Sherman was beginning the march of his army northward to join Grant. It was perhaps not strange that instead of talk about the future, the great Confederate Commander talked with Mosby about his father, Light-Horse Harry Lee. In the American Revolution Light-Horse Harry had been something of a partisan, too. Perhaps Mosby, then only thirty-one, reminded the tired Lee of his father who had fought when he was young, too.

Mosby's men had not been idle while he was away. They wiped out the last of the so-called Loudoun County Rangers, who had sympathized with the Yankees, and had tried by every trick to catch Mosby's band. Still, while the Gray Ghost, always the observant scout, had recognized the critical Confederate situation at Petersburg, he received clearer warning of the desperate state of Reb affairs in a message from Lee in March.

"Collect your command and watch the country from front of Gordonsville to Blue Ridge and also Valley," Lee told him. "Your command is all now in that section."

Nobody understood better than Mosby the hopelessness of a situation in which his 800 men were all the South had to fight with in that area. He collected his men as ordered. He was not surprised, though not yet ready to give up, when word came through the confusion of Virginia that on April 9, 1865, Lee had surrendered at Appomattox.

He secured a copy of a circular put out by the Yankees on April 10. It told of the generous terms Grant had accorded Lee's men. All were free to go home under parole not to take up arms against the United States. Then the official paper added:

"The guerrilla chief Mosby is not included in the parole."

CHAPTER 14

The Undefeated

Mosby's men were in no mood for surrender. They had not been defeated. They were stubbornly ready for more fight if necessary. Some wanted the Gray Ghost to lead his band to Mexico where the Emperor Maximilian, beset by revolutionists, was eager for experienced soldiers. Others hoped that they could slip through Grant's armies and join the Confederate General Joseph E. Johnston, who had not yet surrendered in Carolina. And if Johnston failed they would still be on the road to Mexico.

"I do not intend to remain in the country," Mosby himself said.

Yet he was unwilling as General Lee had been, as he wrote to Federal General W. S. Hancock, "to cause the useless effusion of blood or to inflict upon a war-torn population any unnecessary distress." Also General Grant was as anxious as possible to end the fighting of "all the fragments of the Army of Northern Virginia." Two days after Appomattox, General Grant authorized acceptance of the surrender of Mosby's band on the same conditions offered Lee's men.

Mosby was still reluctant. He had received no official word of Lee's surrender. He was, he said, not sure that the "emergency has arisen which would justify the surrender of my command." He proposed a suspension of hostilities until he could secure the information he felt he needed. He wrote that letter to General Hancock on April 15, which tragically happened to be the day on which Lincoln died of the assassin's bullet.

One of the conspirators with John Wilkes Booth was Lewis Thornton Powell, alias Lewis Payne. He had been a ranger but had deserted to the Yanks. Despite the fact that Payne had deserted Mosby, in the excitement rumors were spread linking the partisan chief with Lincoln's murder. At that moment, Grant grew impatient with Mosby's delay in surrendering.

"If Mosby does not avail himself of the present truce," he told Hancock, "end it and hunt him and his men down. Guerrillas . . . will not be entitled to quarter."

No such hunt was to be necessary. If Mosby declined to surrender his band, he realized that their time of fighting together was over. By the grapevine system of communication he had devised when he kept his men dispersed for safety, he sent out a call for their assembly at the village of Salem on April 21, 1865. In their best uniforms with their pistols shining and their horses curried to perfection, the partisans began to gather soon after dawn. It was a dreary rainy day. The unhappy men waited for their leader. He came late on his beautiful horse, Croquette. Clean-shaven again, he was a slim, impressive figure in his splendid uniform. His boots and pistols gleamed. His men found him more silent than ever.

At noon on a green north of town the companies formed before him. No roll was called but scarcely 200 rangers were present. The Gray Ghost rode to the upper end of the line and slowly moved along it silently regarding the men. Then taking his place before the partisans, he listened as his brother, William H. Mosby, read for him his last message to his men.

"Soldiers: I have summoned you together for the last time. The vision we cherished of a free and independent

country has vanished, and that country is now the spoil of a conqueror.

"I disband your organization in preference to surrendering to our enemies. I am no longer your commander. After an association of more than two eventful years, I part from you with a just pride in the fame of your achievements and grateful recollections of your generous kindness to myself. And now at this moment of bidding you a final adieu, accept the assurance of my unchanging confidence and regard.

"Farewell!"

He rode away. But behind him rumors spread about the activities of the unsurrendered rebel. Rewards were offered for his capture. He hid for a time at the remote farm of an uncle in Nelson County, east of Lexington, where General Lee became head of little Washington College. Lee apparently intervened for Mosby with General Grant. On June 12, in full uniform the partisan rode into Lynchburg to give his parole. There, however, he found that officers, not knowing that it had been agreed to, planned to arrest him. The Gray Ghost flared in anger. He slapped his pistols.

"There are twelve bullets here, gentlemen," he said, "and every last one of them will be fired before you take me."

They did not take him. He rode away. More negotiations went on. Finally at the end of June, he surrendered and was allowed to give his parole. His troubles were not over, however. In August in Alexandria he was involved in a commotion between his Southern friends and Union people. He was put under arrest for two days and released with an order not to come into that section of Virginia again. The months passed. Still in January 1866, he was arrested by Federal soldiers in Lynchburg.

"Don't be uneasy," he wrote Pauline. "Kiss the children for me."

Pauline was impatient with continual uneasiness. She went to Washington and saw General Grant. He received her graciously. He listened to her story. Then in his own handwriting he wrote a letter:

> Hdqrs. Armies of the United States
> Washington, D. C., February 2, 1866.
>
> John S. Mosby, late of the Southern army, will, hereafter, be exempt from arrest by military authorities, except for the violation of his parole, unless directed by the President of the United States, Secretary of War or from these headquarters.
>
> His parole will authorize him to travel freely within the state of Virginia, and as no obstacle has been thrown in the way of paroled officers and men pursuing their civil pursuits, or traveling out of their states, the same privilege will be extended to J. S. Mosby, unless otherwise directed by competent authority.
>
> U. S. Grant

So finally on high authority John Mosby's war with the United States ended almost a year after it had ended for everybody else. He was never docile in surrender, however. Indeed, even in April in Leesburg, he was still the old, proud, ready-to-fight Gray Ghost. Grant's letter did not excuse Mosby from the order that no Confederate buttons or insignia should be worn. So when he appeared in Leesburg in his full uniform with Confederate buttons gleaming on it, a Yankee officer told him to remove them. The ex-partisan let him know there were not enough Yankees in Virginia to make him do it. For a little while it looked as if the war would start all over again about Mosby's buttons. The certain fact is that Mosby won that last fight.

He was not always bristling. Indeed, a Northern newspaperman saw and wrote a picture of the Gray Ghost's gentler side. He told of a solitary man standing in Hollywood Cemetery in Richmond beside the grave of Jeb Stuart. It was early morning. The grave of the great Confederate cavalryman with whom Mosby had begun his gay, fierce riding was then still unmarked. The thin, erect man stood a long time beside the grave. Then he bent over and put a flower on it. The man, of course, was John Mosby.

He was only thirty-one at the war's end. The merry Jeb Stuart would have been, if he had lived, only thirty-two. Yet young men seemed old in the South which had fought four, fierce, desperate years. Gallantry and glory seemed all behind. The job now was the rebuilding of the land for which they had fought. Mosby chose to live at Warrenton, in the midst of the country which Sheridan said would hate him for bringing disaster upon it. It loved him and fought to the last with him instead.

There he nailed up his shingle, "John S. Mosby—Attorney-at-law." It seemed forever since he had come through that town with the first group of fifteen men Jeb Stuart had let him have. Now the crops were green again in the fields which had been burned. New barns were built. Men who had fought with pistols leaned to the plow. In the hills around Mosby's law office lived many of the rangers who had ridden with the Gray Ghost on grim errands in the band which was disbanded forever but never surrendered.

CHAPTER 15

Reunion Forever

To many, John Mosby became as unpredictable in peace as he had been in war. He settled down to the pleasant life of a Virginia gentleman and county seat lawyer. In that country of many fine horses, he kept several beautiful animals from the string he had collected in war. He added racers to his stable. His law practice flourished. Once he seemed the old pistol-ready ranger when he dared the town's military Governor to a duel—which that official ducked. But Mosby shocked all the traditions of Virginia gentlemen when, in the hot post-war politics, the ex-Rebel raider came out for Grant's election to a second term as President.

In May 1872, Southerners were amazed by the news that Mosby had been a visitor at the White House. That was the beginning of what the old partisan called "the fiery ordeal I have been through in supporting Grant." Still he insisted that if the Southern people wanted reconciliation, as they said they did, the logical thing to do was to vote for Grant. Most Southerners violently disagreed. The old Union Commander and the one-time Gray Ghost became fast friends. Undoubtedly Mosby remembered Grant's kind reception of Pauline. Both liked to joke about the time when Mosby narrowly missed capturing the Union General.

"If I had captured you," Mosby told the President, "things might have changed—I might have been in the

White House and you might be calling on me."

"Yes," Grant agreed grinning.

Feeling grew stronger against Mosby even among his old friends when he helped win the vote of Virginia for Grant. In the heated politics which followed, Mosby was arrested to prevent his participation in a duel. Southern editors denounced him. One night in the bitter contest between Rutherford B. Hayes and Samuel Tilden for the Presidency, as Mosby stepped off the train in Warrenton someone shot at him from the dark. During his last days in the White House Grant began to fear for the safety of his friend. Mosby had never accepted office from Grant but the General asked his successor, President Hayes, to appoint the still combative raider United States Consul to Hong Kong.

No fighting man had ever been able to drive Mosby from the Virginia country he loved. But now bitterness grew about him. He was lonely. Pauline died on May 10, 1876. The Gray Ghost began to be gray indeed. He served four years in China. Then he came home to a position the dying Grant had secured for him as attorney with the Southern Pacific Railroad. Later he held positions in the government at Washington. He began to lecture and write about his war experiences. In defending the course of Jeb Stuart in the Gettysburg campaign, Mosby wrote almost as if he were leading a charge against armed enemies.

The years passed. The boy, who it was feared would never grow to maturity, became an old man. He survived a nearly fatal accident at the age of sixty-three when a runaway horse kicked him in the face. Sometimes as he grew older he expressed the wish that he could have died fighting with his men. They gathered in reunions, marked by laughter and tears. Many of the rangers had become distinguished men, some eminent preachers.

"Well, boys," Mosby told them, "if you fight the devil

like you fought the Yankees, there will be something to record on Judgment Day."

He became popular as writer and speaker among the Yankees he had fought. And at last even Virginia forgave him his post-war politics. The University of Virginia, from which as a frail, belligerent boy he had been expelled, presented him with a medal and its praise: "Endowed with the gift of friendship, which won for you the confidence of both Lee and Grant, you have proven yourself a man of war, a man of letters, and a man of affairs worthy of the best traditions of your university and your state, to both of which you have been a loyal son."

He was old and poor when he died in Washington in 1916 at the age of 82. It was Memorial Day and America would in less than a year enter World War I. He was buried in Warrenton beside Pauline and near the graves of partisans who had fallen fighting by his side half a century before. Virginia was quiet and warm and green around his grave. The day seemed fitting for a last song of the rangers, which had been read at one of their hilarious and misty-eyed reunions:

> The circling seasons come and go,
>   Springs dawn and autumns set,
> And winter, with its drifted snow,
>   Repays the summer's debt:
> And song of birds and hint of bloom
>   Are gay and bright as when,
> Those gallant lads rode to their doom
>   Long since with Mosby's men.

At last and once again, their leader forever, John Mosby had joined the gallant boys of his band.